THE EMMAUS REPORT

Publishers of *The Emmaus Report*

Australia

Anglican Information Office
St Andrew's House
Sydney Square
Sydney 2000

Canada

Anglican Book Centre
600 Jarvis Street
Toronto, Ontario M4Y 2J6

Ghana

Anglican Printing Press
PO Box 8
Accra

India

ISPCK
PO Box 1585
Kashmere Gate
Delhi 11006

Kenya

Uzima Press Ltd
PO Box 48127
Nairobi

New Zealand

Collins Liturgical Publications
PO Box 1
Auckland

Nigeria

CSS Press
50 Broad Street
PO Box 174
Lagos

Southern and Central Africa

Collins Liturgical Publications
Distributed in Southern
Africa by
Lux Verbi, PO Box 1822
Cape Town 8000

Tanzania

Central Tanganyika Press
PO Box 15
Dodoma

Uganda

Centenary Publishing House
PO Box 2776
Kampala

United Kingdom

Church House Publishing
Church House
Great Smith Street
London SW1P 3NZ

United States of America

Forward Movement Publications
412 Sycamore Street
Cincinnati, Ohio 45202

THE EMMAUS REPORT

A report of the
Anglican Ecumenical Consultation
which took place at
The Emmaus Retreat Centre,
West Wickham, Kent, England

27 January – 2 February 1987

in preparation for
ACC-7, Singapore, 1987
and
The Lambeth Conference 1988

PUBLISHED FOR THE
ANGLICAN CONSULTATIVE COUNCIL

Published 1987 for the Anglican Consultative Council, 14 Great Peter Street, London SW1P 3NQ.

This edition by
**Church House Publishing,
Church House, Great Smith Street,
London SW1P 3NZ**

ISBN 0 7151 4763 3

Printed by Tas Print, George Lane, South Woodford, London E18.

Contents

Preface

At the end of January 1987 the Chairman and Vice-Chairman chosen to lead the Ecumenical Relations section at the Lambeth Conference 1988 met for five days with a number of bishops and ecumenical officers from the Anglican Communion.

The meeting had two purposes. It was to prepare a document for the Ecumenical Relations section at Lambeth. It was also to prepare a paper on Ecumenical Relations for ACC-7. The original intention was that the same paper should serve both purposes. However the time proved insufficient to produce a complete document for Lambeth 1988, and so the Chairman and Vice-Chairman will meet at the end of July 1987 with one or two others to supplement the present document. The advantage of this will be that they will be able to incorporate into their final preparatory document comments that come from ACC-7, and responses to the letter that they sent earlier to the bishops who will come to Canterbury in 1988.

The present document, prepared for ACC-7 contains the following:

1. Christian Unity; the Gift, the Vision and the Way.
    Differing Contexts and Agenda
    The Role of the Lambeth Conference and the Unity of the Anglican Communion
    The Reality of Unity
    The Vision of Unity
    A provisional examination of terms

2. Churches in Full Communion

3. The Anglican-Roman Catholic International Commission:
    The Final Report:
    History
    The Goal
    Methodology
    Reception and Response
    Particular Issues

In addition, those who met at the Emmaus Centre began to draft material for the 1988 Lambeth Conference on Local Ecumenism (11), on the Unity We Seek in Diversity (12), on a Vision of Unity and on Steps on the Way. This material, together possibly with a consideration of the role of Councils of Churches and other ecumenical issues, will be available for inclusion in the final preparatory document.

What follows in this document, which is directed to ACC-7, includes the draft of 1–8 and 10 above, together with an account of the visit to the Ecumenical Centre in Geneva of some members of the group which prepared the rest of the document. The account of this visit is clearly related to 9 above. 10 is directed especially to ACC-7. Considerable work has been done on 11 and 12, but those parts were judged neither ready nor totally apposite to be sent to ACC-7.

What in the following pages appear to be the particular issues which we ask ACC-7 to consider?

Chapter 2 on Churches in Full Communion presents a challenge to Anglicans. Are we prepared to offer full membership of the Anglican Communion to the United Churches of the Indian subcontinent and any new United Churches which may be formed partly from existing Anglican Provinces? Should 'full communion' mean more than full interchangeability of ministries and members? Should it also include organs of consultation and joint decision-making?

Chapter 3 on the ARCIC *Final Report* is prepared primarily for Lambeth 1988 to pronounce the consensus of the Anglican Communion. However not all Provinces have yet sent in their Response to the ACC. Can the members of ACC-7 whose Provinces have not yet issued their Response manage to elicit one as soon as possible? The ACC will also wish to consider commending the first statement of ARCIC II, *Salvation and the Church,* to the Provinces.

Chapter 4 on Changes in Anglican-Lutheran Relations raises the question of what it means to be in 'full communion'. It also describes the interim relationship, short of full communion, which now exists between the Episcopal and Lutheran Churches in the USA. The Church of England has very recently taken the first step towards establishing a similar relationship with the Evangelical Church in Germany in the Federal Republic of Germany and with the Federation Evangelical Churches in the German Democratic Republic. Such 'interim eucharistic sharing' allows some sharing of ministry but not full interchangeability of ministries. Does ACC continue to support this significant step on the way to full communion?

Chapter 5 on Anglican-Orthodox Relations presents three challenges to ACC-7. The Orthodox Churches will expect the Lambeth Conference to make a statement on behalf of the Anglican Communion about the Filioque. Have the Provinces come to a sufficiently clear mind on this issue to enable the Lambeth Bishops in 1988 to make such a statement? If not, can those Provinces, which have as yet not made a statement or decision, consider the matter before Lambeth 1988? The second challenge is inherent in the different status accorded to the two Agreed Statements in the two Communions. From the moment the Statements were signed by the Orthodox delegates they had official status in Orthodox Churches. How does ACC-7 suggest the Anglican Communion should adopt these Statements or the appropriate parts of them, as representing its official position? The third challenge is the need for a clarification of the direction of this, the largest and oldest of the international theological dialogues. One of its goals in the eyes of the Orthodox appears to have been an examination of Anglican faith and order to discover if it is sufficiently Orthodox for full unity to be established with the Anglican Communion. How do the Anglicans on their part see the goal of the theological dialogue? Is further mutual clarification of the goal possible? What relation does the international dialogue have to local and regional dialogue and pastoral exchange?

Although Anglicans have had a long history of good relations with the Oriental Orthodox Churches, 1985 marked the beginning of a more formal exchange. Chapter 6 on Anglican-Oriental Orthodox Relations reminds Anglicans of many of the deepest differences which threaten to break God's world asunder, for the Oriental Orthodox Churches exist in Marxist and atheist states, or where Islam and Christianity find themselves on different sides of deep political divisions, or in Ethiopia where they struggled to cope with famine. Mutual support and pastoral care of one another's people in dispersion is clearly required. Will ACC-7 also support the inclusion of theological and ecclesiological concerns in the Forum?

Chapter 7 on Anglican-Reformed Relations shows the relationship between the unity of humanity in God's Kingdom and the unity of the Church in his design. *God's Reign and Our Unity* is one of the most frequently quoted of the International Dialogue Reports both for what it says about the relationship of Church and Kingdom and for what it says about the Goal of Unity. So far however it has been referred to local and regional consideration, and there is little in the way of formal response from Provinces. How can ACC-7 help the bishops at Lambeth 1988 to locate in Anglican thought generally the very important issues tackled in *God's Reign and Our Unity?*

Chapter 8 on the Responses of the Anglican Communion to *Baptism, Eucharist and Ministry* sets this multilateral dialogue report in relation to all the dialogues and in the context of all the other work planned or proceeding under the auspices of the Faith and Order Commission. The value of comparing the responses of all Anglican Provinces to BEM (a process not originally envisaged by the World Council of Churches) is commended. This Chapter concludes with issues for ACC-7 to consider (paragraph 51).

Because of the production of so many reports from international theological dialogues there is a danger that ACC-7 and the Lambeth Conference may focus exclusively on these. That is why a supplementary report is required to show that there are other vital aspects of ecumenism. An issue facing all the Churches, and not only ACC-7, is to discover the appropriate relationship between the unity of the Churches and the search for Justice, Peace and the Integrity of Creation.

The Growth of New Churches presents a challenge which takes a different form in different Provinces, and which is more acute in some than in others. It invites ACC-7 to gather resources to help the Communion meet this challenge.

ACC-7 might helpfully consider what other aspects of ecumenical work should be tackled by the bishops as they meet at Lambeth in 1988.

The overall question which the document for Lambeth 1988 will tackle is where are we in the ecumenical movement today, and where are we going.

Martin Reardon

March 1987

(This report was received and commended by ACC-7: Singapore 1987.)

1

Christian Unity: The Gift, the Vision and the Way

Introduction: Differing Contexts and Agenda

The word 'ecumenical' means 'relating' to the whole inhabited world'. The modern ecumenical movement therefore should not be confined to the internal unity of the Christian Churches, let alone to doctrinal discussions among western Churches. Properly understood it concerns the Church's participating in the work of God in reconciling the whole world through Jesus Christ.

It is not possible for any individual Christian or Province to grasp the fulness of this ecumenical vision or to see clearly the goal of Christian unity. Some may focus on the search for doctrinal agreement. Others may be more concerned with practical co-operation. Some may be pre-occupied with the reconciliation of denominations. Others may be primarily concerned with the reconciliation in Christ of those different races within their own Church, or between those who have wealth and influence and those who have none. All these tasks, and many others, may properly be seen to be part of the one ecumenical movement.

Such differing ecumenical priorities exist among the individual members of each of our Provinces, and the search for consensus and the fulness of the ecumenical vision is as much a matter for discussion between Anglicans in the same Province, as between Anglicans and members of other Christian Churches.

However, as we prepare for the coming together of bishops from all parts of the Anglican Communion in the Lambeth

Conference, it is important to realise that each Province (and to a certain extent each diocese) has its own distinctive history, its own social and cultural setting, its own particular ecumenical agenda. Some Provinces which comprise large, national Churches may look forward without fear to an organic union of Churches sprung from different traditions. Some Provinces which consist of small, minority Churches may find such a goal very hard to contemplate as they try to preserve a distinctively Anglican witness. Other Provinces, where many different Churches of similar size and standing exist side by side, may search rather for co-operation in a diversified kind of unity. Moreover, we have to recognise that the Churches in the British Isles and North America have transferred their own ecclesiastical divisions to the Third World. There, separated from their historical and theological roots, they have proved even more difficult to deal with, and they have sometimes made existing tribal or racial divisions worse.

If the members of the Anglican Communion are to share a common ecumenical vision, they have to begin by understanding one another's differing circumstances, attitudes and agenda.

In this preparatory document it is not possible to examine each Provincial situation one by one in detail; but when they are at the Lambeth Conference it will be important for the bishops to listen not only to what those from other Provinces say, but also to try to understand something of the background from which they say it.

One experience which many Provinces have shared in the last two decades has been the failure of a scheme of union or proposals for a covenant of unity with local Protestant Churches at national or Provincial level. These failures often led to disillusionment with the ecumenical movement and to a loss of momentum. The ecumenical ship seemed becalmed, and many Christians turned their attention to other matters which appeared to them to have a higher priority and more immediate hope of success.

However we also discern remarkable signs of hope. Some Provinces, notably Wales, have persevered with their unity

7

proposals, even when they may have experienced a loss of momentum. They have taken out the oars and are rowing.

A remarkable sign of hope is the publication of the reports of five international, ecumenical dialogues during the first five years of this decade. Although each of these dialogues has a different background and tackles the particular disagreements which have marked the separation of particular Churches, nevertheless, taken as a whole, the dialogues show such a remarkable convergence in matters of faith and Church order as could not have been conceived even twenty years ago.

Another sign of hope has been the growing international Christian support for those suffering from racial discrimination and oppression, for example, in South Africa.

Another sign of hope has been the renewal and expansion in membership of a number of conciliar ecumenical bodies in different parts of the world. For example the Council of Churches in New Zealand has been replaced by the Conference which now includes Roman Catholics and Pentecostals. In Great Britain a million people took part in a Lent Course in 1986 on the nature and purpose of the Church in the world. This was part of a process to discover how a much wider range of Christian Churches than ever before, including the Roman Catholic and black-led Churches, might work and pray together more effectively.

In North America and in many other places, when Christians worship in one another's Churches they have begun to feel at home. People of different Christian traditions engage together in community service among the poor. They feel they belong together, so that in a rapidly growing number of places Christian congregations of different traditions have committed themselves to pray, to study and to work together as one people engaged in the one mission of the one God to one world.

Thus despite setbacks the ecumenical movement is growing rapidly and quietly at the international, national and local levels at the same time.

In this document we attempt to describe the ecumenical scene as it presents itself to the Anglican Communion today.

Nevertheless we do not start from scratch. Successive Lambeth Conferences have made important statements about the ecumenical movement. Before we consider in detail certain developments which have taken place in the decade since Lambeth 1978, it may be helpful to try to do two things:

(1) to summarise briefly what has been the remarkably consistent, though developing, teaching of Lambeth Conferences over the last 100 years since the Chicago–Lambeth Quadrilateral was first put forward;

(2) to attempt a provisional definition of some of the terms used to describe the goal of unity.

Before even doing these two things it will be necessary to consider how the wider goal of universal unity sought by the Lambeth bishops relates to the unity of the Anglican Communion itself.

The Role of the Lambeth Conference and the Unity of the Anglican Communion

Before considering what successive Lambeth Conferences have said about the general goal of unity, it is instructive to see how the assembled bishops regarded their own meeting and the status of the Anglican Communion. For during the last 120 years the Anglican Communion has developed from a few white and predominantly English-speaking Churches and their missions, without any global organisation, to a world-wide Communion growing together into a universal Church. This development has been made by Church leaders at the same time committed to the goal of a wider unity.

In an opening address to the first Lambeth Conference on 24th September, 1867, Archbishop Longley said:

> It has never been contemplated that we should assume the functions of a general synod of all the Churches in full communion with the Church of England, and take upon ourselves to enact canons that should be binding upon those here represented. We merely propose to discuss matters of practical interest and pronounce what we deem expedient in resolutions which may serve as safe guides to future action. (*Lambeth Conferences 1867-1930,* SPCK, 1948, p.9).

9

However, it was the first Lambeth Conference which achieved a system of Provincial organisation for the Anglican Communion, and this has remained a feature of Anglican order ever since.

In 1878 the Second Lambeth Conference set out what it called 'Principles of Church Order' governing the interchange of clergy between Provinces and dioceses; and it also laid down guidelines for the establishment of 'Provincial and Diocesan Courts of Discipline' (*ibid.* pp. 286f).

As early as the Fourth Lambeth Conference in 1897 the Bishops expressed their abhorrence of the idea of parallel jurisdictions existing in the same geographical area (Res. 24 *ibid.* p 288). This Resolution was re-affirmed in Resolution 22 of the 1908 Lambeth Conference which stated:

> . . . the principle of one Bishop for one area is the ideal to be aimed at as the best means of securing the unity of all races and nations in the Holy Catholic Church. (*Lambeth Conferences 1867-1930*, p. 289).

Since then this view has been consistently put forward as the ideal, though it has been increasingly realised that in the complexities of modern society there may be a case for multiple jurisdictions so long as they are exercised in full collegiality. *Lambeth 1968* (p. 125) commended Chapter III of *Intercommunion Today* (CIO, 1968). In that Report we find the following:

> This unity of the local Church has in the past been represented by the rule which allows only one bishop in one place, the whole family united round the father of the family. There may be national reasons (as in the relationship between different rites within the Roman Catholic Church), or historical reasons . . . which make it necessary to bear the anomaly of two overlapping communities in the same area, for a greater or lesser time, and in the future development of urban societies it may be that geographical considerations will be less influential in the ordering of the Church's life than they have been in the past. It will be increasingly difficult to define the nature of 'one place'. At the present time, however, there seem to be many reasons to maintain the historical practice. (*ibid.* p. 18).

The 1968 Conference 'deplored the existence of parallel jurisdictions in Europe' (Resolution 63). The 1978 Conference noted that a solution to the problem in Europe had not been found and called for a 'greater emphasis' on the positive efforts to find a solution.

Meanwhile ECUSA and the Provinces of New Zealand and Southern Africa have each appointed bishops (Navajo, Aotearoa, and the Order of Ethiopia respectively) in collegiality with their fellow bishops to minister to ethnic groups.

The Conference of 1920 tried to describe its own status:

> The Lambeth Conference . . . does not claim to exercise any powers of control or command. It stands for the far more spiritual and more Christian principle of loyalty to the fellowship. The Churches represented in it are indeed independent, but independent with the Christian freedom which recognises the restraints of truth and love. They are not free to deny the truth. They are not free to ignore the fellowship . . . the Conference is . . . a fellowship in the Spirit. (*Encyclical Letter, ibid.* p. 14).

The Committee on Reunion of the 1920 Conference described the change that had taken place in the Anglican Communion since the first Lambeth Conference:

> At the date of the first Lambeth Conference, 1867, this Communion had taken the form of a federation of self-governing Churches, held together for the most part without legal sanctions by a common reverence for the same traditions and a common use of a Prayer Book . . . the Anglican Communion of today is a federation of Churches, some national, some regional, but no longer predominantly Anglo-Saxon in race, nor can it be expected that it will attach special value to Anglo-Saxon traditions . . . It already presents an example on a small scale of the problems which attach to the unity of a Universal Church. As the years go on, its ideals must become less Anglican and more Catholic. It cannot look to any bonds of union holding it together, other than those which should hold together the Catholic Church itself. (*Lambeth Conference 1920,* SPCK, p. 137).

This quotation shows that Anglican attempts to preserve and increase the unity of the Anglican Communion should not be too clearly distinguished from Anglican attempts to look

forward to the unity of the whole Church. Both the Lambeth
Conference of 1878 and that of 1930 tackle the issue of the unity
of the Anglican Communion in the context of an explicit desire
for the reunion of the whole Christian Church.

The 1878 statement specifically affirmed that the Church of
England had always been ready to resort to the assembling of a
'true General Council' of all the Churches of Christ.

The desire for the calling of a truly universal council was
affirmed in the 1968 Lambeth Conference (Resolution 44) and
re-affirmed in the 1978 Lambeth Conference.

The Encyclical Letter of the 1930 Conference contained the
following:

> (The Anglican) Communion is a commonwealth of Churches
> without a central constitution: it is a federation without a federal
> government . . . They are, in the idiom of our fathers, 'particular or
> national' Churches, and they repudiate any idea of a central
> authority, other than Councils of Bishops. (*ibid.* p. 155) (2).

The decentralised nature of the Anglican Communion was
considered further in 1948 when the Committee on The
Anglican Communion recalled that 'Former Lambeth
Conferences have wisely rejected proposals for a formal
primacy of Canterbury, for an Appellate Tribunal, and for
giving the Conference the status of a legislative synod'. The
Committee report goes on to consider the 'dispersed' rather
than 'centralised' nature of authority in the Anglican
Communion. The Committee's statement on, 'The Meaning
and Unity of the Anglican Communion' (*Lambeth 1948,*
SPCK, pp. II. 84–86) remains a classic presentation of the
Anglican position, but it has been complemented in recent
years by a growing concern about what holds the Communion
together. In 1968 the Lambeth Conference met after the
Second Vatican Council and immediately after the Uppsala
Assembly of the World Council of Churches. The Lambeth
Conference section on Renewal in Unity dealt with
'Episcopacy, Collegiality and Papacy'.

> Within the college of bishops it is evident that there must be a
> president. In the Anglican Communion this position is at present
> held by the occupant of the historic see of Canterbury, who enjoys

a primacy of honour, not of jurisdiction. This primacy is found to involve, in a particular way, that care of all the Churches which is shared by all the bishops. (*Lambeth,* 1968, p. 137).

The 1968 Lambeth Conference recommended the establishment of the Anglican Consultative Council. This was formed and had held three meetings before 1978. The 1978 Lambeth Conference instituted a further set of regular meetings, that of the Anglican Primates; and asked that consideration should be given to the inter-relationship of the Conference, the Council, the Primates' Meeting and the Archbishop of Canterbury himself (Resolution 12). In a statement on the basis of Anglican unity it speaks of 'the patterning of elements shared in common with other Churches'. After listing several of these elements it concludes:

It is personally grounded in the loyal relationship of each of the Churches to the Archbishop of Canterbury who is freely recognised as the focus of unity. (*Lambeth* 1978, CIO, p. 98).

The same Conference asked that an Inter-Anglican Theological and Doctrinal Commission should be set up (Resolution 25). It asked the Anglican Consultative Council, in consultation with other Churches, to formulate appropriate definitions of terms used in inter-Church relations (Resolution 30). It also devoted a great deal of time to the issue of women in the priesthood and the episcopate, an issue on which there was wide divergence of opinion, and which was therefore a test of the will and ability of the Communion to hold together.

The Communion was also faced with coming to a common mind on the reports of various bilateral dialogues. The Fifth Meeting of the Anglican Consultative Council, held at Newcastle upon Tyne in 1981, asked:

How is it possible for a Communion of autonomous Provincial Churches to come to a common acceptance of an ecumenical agreement? The Council is quite clear that the formal acceptance of any ecumenical agreement remains with the Provincial Synods of the Communion. But the question then arises as to how and where an overall consensus is to be discerned and pronounced . . . We believe the Lambeth Conference will be best able to discern and pronounce a consensus. (*ACC-5,* 1981, ACC, p.43).

This and other factors have led to the creation of a more complex machinery to enable the Provinces to work together. Professor John Macquarrie, speaking at Lambeth 1978, referred to the independence of the Provinces of the Communion:

> . . . I am not much impressed with the idea of an autonomous Church. This is especially the case at a time when we hear a great deal of talk about collegiality, partnership, conciliarity, and so on. If these are not just empty words that are bandied about, if they stand for a real desire to share experience and decision-making, then each so-called autonomous Church ought to be in constant consultation with its sister Churches.

Canon Samuel Van Culin listed the major elements of the present inter-Anglican organisation when he delivered his address as Secretary General to the Sixth Meeting of the Anglican Consultative Council in Lagos in 1984. He commented:

> The Provinces are of course autonomous but inter-dependent. The structure and relationships which express and carry this inter-dependence are only gradually developing. Only when such structures and relationships exist, not only for the Anglican Communion, but also for the wider Church as a whole, shall we know what full communion and organic union might really mean. (*Bonds of Affection, Proceedings of ACC-6,* ACC, 1984, p.8).

The Lambeth bishops have been clear that the Anglican Communion is looking forward to a wider unity. This vision was clear in their readiness to participate in a true General Council of all the Churches of Christ. This vision has also fuelled the search for a wider episcopal fellowship. It has given impetus to the continued pre-occupation with the search for Christian unity. It was expressed, for example, in 1930, in the following way:

> . . . in its present character we believe that (the Anglican Communion) is transitional, and we forecast the day when the racial and historical connections which at present characterise it will be transcended and the life of our Communion will be merged in a larger fellowship in the Catholic Church. (*Lambeth,* 1930, p.153).

The vision of the 1948 Conference was of the provisional and incomplete nature of the present Anglican Communion, which was seen as 'a portion of the Holy Catholic Church', and of its ultimate fusion with other traditions, and their transformation into a wider unity in one Church. However, it warned that this vision is still far from its attainment.

> It would be . . . a betrayal of our trust before God if the Anglican Communion were to allow itself to be dispersed before its particular work was done. (*ibid*. p.123).

The Reality of Unity

The 1897 Lambeth Conference in Resolution 34 stated:

> that every opportunity be taken to emphasise the Divine purpose of visible unity among Christians, as a fact of revelation.

This Resolution was re-affirmed in 1908.

However, it was the *Encyclical Letter* of the 1920 Conference which affirmed that unity was not simply a human goal to be sought, but a divine reality to be realised.

> In this Appeal we urge . . . a new approach to reunion; to adopt a new point of view; to look up to the reality as it is in God. The unity we seek exists. It is in God, who is the perfection of unity, the one Father, the one Lord, the one Spirit, Who gives life to the one Body. Again, the one Body exists. It needs not to be made nor to be remade, but to become organic and visible. Once more the fellowship of the members of the one Body exists. It is the work of God, not of man. We have only to discover it, and to set free its activities. (*Lambeth*, 1920, SPCK, 1920, p. 12).

In the light of this the 1958 Lambeth Conference affirmed our given baptismal unity:

> We believe in One, Holy Catholic, and Apostolic Church, which takes its origin not in the will of man but in the will of our Lord Jesus Christ. All those who believe in our Lord Jesus Christ and have been baptised in the name of the Holy Trinity are incorporated into the Body of Christ and are members of the Church. Here is a unity already given.

The 1968 Conference traces the unity of Christians to the Unity of the Trinity:

> The unity of God with man and of men with one another is rooted in the mystery of the unity of the Godhead . . .

15

It goes on to describe the calling of the Church in God's plan for the universe:

> So the Church is called to be the foretaste of a redeemed creation, a sign of the coming unity of mankind, a pointer to the time when God shall be all in all. We may not speak of the limited task of manifesting a greater unity between separated Christians here and now unless we always do so in this context of the unfathomable unity of the Godhead, communicated by the Spirit as the Church is renewed in all its members in holiness and truth for mission and service to all mankind and as it awaits the final summing up of all things in Christ . . . The unity which is God's gift is indestructible because it is rooted in Christ's once-for-all reconciliation.
>
> (*Lambeth 1968*, SPCK, p. 122).

The Vision of Unity

The 1888 Lambeth Conference earnestly requested

> the constituted authorities . . . of our Communion . . . to enter into brotherly conference . . . with representatives of other Christian Communions . . . in order to consider what steps can be taken, either towards corporate Reunion, or towards such relation as may prepare the way for fuller organic unity hereafter (*Resolution* 12).

In this context 'corporate Reunion' appears to mean the same thing as 'organic unity', that is the complete and living unity of two or more communions in one body.

It was the 1888 Conference which took over from the General Convention of the American Episcopal Church, held in Chicago in 1886, what came to be called the 'Lambeth Quadrilateral' (see *The Chicago-Lambeth Quadrilateral*, ACC, 1984). This was put forward as 'a basis on which approach may be by God's blessing made towards Home Reunion' (*Resolution* 11). The Quadrilateral was intended as a basis for discussion, not as an all-sufficient outline of all that would be required for a united Church.

The 1897 Lambeth Conference emphasised 'the Divine purpose of visible unity among Christians' (*Resolution* 34).

The 1908 Lambeth Conference reaffirmed this Resolution. It affirmed:

that in all partial projects of reunion and intercommunion the final attainment of the divine purpose should be kept in view as our object; and that care should be taken to do what will advance the reunion of the whole of Christendom. (*Resolution* 38).

Of particular significance today is the affirmation of the 1908 Conference that:

All races and peoples, whatever their language or conditions, must be welded into one Body, and the organisation of different races living side by side into separate or independent Churches, on the basis of race or colour, is inconsistent with the vital and essential principle of the unity of Christ's Church. (*Resolution* 20).

It was, however, the 1920 Lambeth Conference which made the most profound contribution to the ecumenical movement. It followed the fierce debate about the Kikuyu proposal of 1913 for united Christian action in East Africa. It was feared that the heat of this debate would prevent the bishops agreeing on the theme of Christian unity. Archbishop Lang, who chaired the committee on Reunion in 1920 wrote to Parker:

I took the line from the first that it was useless to consider projects and proposals in different parts of the world until we had agreed upon the ideal of unity that we must seek . . .

(*Cosmo Gordon Lang,* J. G. Lockhart, p. 268).

In the *Encyclical Letter* sent out by the bishops from the Conference, it is said that many proposals about the nature of unity were considered – 'Mutual recognition, organic union, federation, absorption, submission'. After the passage already quoted above, about the reality of unity that already exists in God, the Encyclical sets out something of the nature of reunion:

Terms of reunion must no longer be judged by the success with which they meet the claims and preserve the positions of two or more uniting Communions, but by their correspondence to the common ideal of the Church as God would have it to be. Again, in the past, negotiations for reunion have often started with the attempt to define the measure of uniformity which is essential. The impression has been given that nothing else matters. Now we see that those elements of truth about which differences have arisen are essential to the fullness of the witness of the whole church. We have no need to belittle what is distinctive in our own interpretation of

17

Christian life: we believe that it is something precious which we hold in trust for the common good. We desire that others should share in our heritage and our blessings, as we wish to share in theirs. It is not reducing the different groups of Christians to uniformity, but by rightly using their diversity, that the Church can become all things to all men. So long as there is vital connexion with the Head, there is positive value in the differentiation of the members. But we are convinced that this ideal cannot be fulfilled if these groups are content to remain in separation from one another or to be joined together only in some vague federation. Their value for the fullness of Christian life, truth and witness can only be realised if they are united in the fellowship of one visible society whose members are bound together by the ties of a common faith, common sacraments, and a common ministry. It is towards this ideal of a united and truly Catholic Church that we must all set our minds.

This truer conception of the Church and of the Divine purpose disclosed in its history must regulate our aspirations as well as our endeavours. We cannot suppose, indeed, that we have found a way to solve all difficulties in a moment. The vision must become clear to the general body of Christian men and women, and this will take time. We must all direct our gaze towards it. We must help one another to see what steps lead towards its fulfilment, and what steps lead the other way. The vision points the road to reunion. That road may not be short, but, we believe, it will be sure.

It is significant that 'fellowship' is the word which underlies the whole concept of unity. It is the word (in its Greek form, *koinonia*), which the Anglican-Roman Catholic Commission will also choose more than 50 years later. The visibility to the world of this united fellowship should exist, but does not. This separation and division has prevented Christians from fighting worthily 'the battle of the Kingdom', and from growing into the 'fullness of the life in Christ'. What is required is a Church

within whose visible unity all the treasures of faith and order, bequeathed as a heritage by the past to the present, shall be possessed in common, and made serviceable to the Whole Body of Christ. Within this unity Christian Communions now separated from one another would retain much that has long been distinctive in their methods of worship and service. It is through a rich diversity of life and devotion that the unity of the whole fellowship will be fulfilled.

After outlining, in a modified form, the Chicago-Lambeth Quadrilateral, the wholehearted acceptance of which will be involved in the recovery of visible unity, it concentrates on the fourth element, 'a ministry acknowledged by every part of the Church'. It claims that the Episcopate, exercised in a representative and constitutional manner, is the one means of providing such a ministry, and that it is the best instrument for maintaining the unity and continuity of the Church. It does not ask anyone to repudiate his past ministry.

Finally the Resolution asks for 'each group' or Communion to be 'prepared to make sacrifices for the sake of a common fellowship, a common ministry, and a common service to the world'. However, it does 'not ask that any one Communion should consent to be absorbed in another'.

Resolution 9, the 'Appeal to All Christian People', was adopted with almost complete unanimity by the Conference, and is presumably to be interpreted in the light of the report of the Committee on Reunion. From this it is clear that 'organic union' is still the goal, but an organic union in which a diversity of gifts is shared among the members. As we have seen above, the Encyclical letter rejects both 'uniformity' and 'a vague federation'. It is clearly envisaged that a united Church would be episcopal, and one of the primary roles of bishops is that, both individually and as a college, they should act as guardians of unity.

The underlying concept of Christian unity put forward by Lambeth 1920 is that it is fundamentally a reality in God, given to the Church by Jesus Christ and the Holy Spirit, and that the Anglican Communion and other Churches have the task of realising this more faithfully and expressing it more adequately in the unity both given and willed by God. Therefore Lambeth 1920 is able to affirm that it does not

call in question for a moment the spiritual reality of the ministries of those Communions which do not possess the Episcopate. On the contrary we thankfully acknowledge that these ministries have been manifestly blessed and owned by the Holy Spirit as effective means of grace.

However, if these ministries are to become part of a united Church they should be brought into relationship with the historic episcopate for the maintenance of unity and continuity.

The 1930 Lambeth Conference met shortly after the publication of the proposals for a United Church in South India. The Committee on the Unity of the Church took up from 1920 the concept that:

> during the period of division each of the bodies (i.e. Churches) thus separated has under the guidance of the Holy Spirit developed spiritual resources and enjoyed spiritual treasures which must be conserved in the re-united Church, for they are the gift of Christ given to each in its own measure. We must not, for the sake of union, barter away our special heritage, for we hold it in trust for the whole Body of Christ . . .'.

The Committee went on to express the hope

> that through the restoration of union there will come an increase of spiritual life, and that the attainment of further fellowship through union must both enrich each uniting Church by bringing to it a fuller share in the gifts of others, and also enhance and sanctify the gifts brought by each to the common life. (*Lambeth 1930,* SPCK, p. 112).

The Committee then expanded upon the role of the episcopate as one of the treasures which Anglicans have to bring to a united Church.

The goal of a united Church is still clearly described in terms of 'one organic unity' or 'full organic union'.

> . . . we cannot enter into any scheme of federation, involving interchangeability of ministries, while differences on points of order that we think essential still remain. (*ibid*. p. 113).

This unity is clearly envisaged as including a considerable element of organisational unity.

> We cannot regard the maintenance of separately organised Churches as a matter indifferent or unimportant. The will and intention to preserve the unity of the Spirit in the Body of Christ must of necessity underlie all its organisation; and where that unity has been broken, the earnest desire to restore union makes possible a recognition by the Church, in some respects, of ministries which, in separation, must stand on a different footing.

This doctrine of unity-by-desire has been an important feature of Anglican work for unity. Although the general rule is that communion is the goal of unity, and not a means to that goal, an earnest desire for and commitment to the goal of unity may be a reason for some measure of intercommunion.

Present at the 1930 Lambeth Conference were three bishops of the Old Catholic Church in Holland. As a result of this visit a joint Doctrinal Commission was appointed to enter into formal negotiations with a view to intercommunion. In 1931 in Bonn, on the 2nd July, the *Agreement of Bonn* was drawn up;

1.   Each Communion recognises the catholicity and independence of the other, and maintains its own.

2.   Each Communion agrees to permit members of the other Communion to participate in the Sacraments.

3.   Intercommunion does not require from either Communion the acceptance of all doctrinal opinion, sacramental devotion, or liturgical practice characteristic of the other, but implies that each believes the other to hold all the essentials of the Christian Faith.

It is important to note that the Agreement was about 'intercommunion', not 'full communion' as most Anglicans normally say today. The Agreement falls far short of organic union. There is no continuing organisation of arrangement for consultation laid down.

The 1948 Lambeth Conference was faced with a complicated set of union schemes, and proposals for co-operation and intercommunion short of full union. It recognised that schemes for organic union achieved locally, (i.e. nationally or regionally) would encourage other such schemes, and so be 'a definite step towards our ultimate goal'. However, it also recognised that they could lead temporarily to a breach of full communion, and they would inevitably withdraw Provinces from the Anglican Communion. They might even isolate small Churches from the Communions of which their members had formed an integral part. On the other hand the committee was quite clear that in any schemes which fell short of complete union

it is vitally important that organic union should be accepted as the
final objective. (*Lambeth 1948,* SPCK, p. 54).

This reference applied particularly to Archbishop Fisher's
proposal in his Cambridge Sermon of November 1946, that
the English Free Churches might take episcopacy into their
system, and 'grow to full communion with each other before
we start to write a constitution'.

Much of the time of the Committee was devoted to the
vexed problem of the creation of a mutually recognised
ministry, and to that end it produced 'Some principles to guide
further progress' (*Lambeth 1948,* SPCK p. 63 f).

The theme of the 1958 Lambeth Conference was
'reconciliation'. In its Message it affirmed that

A divided Church cannot heal the wounds of a divided world.
Therefore our most urgent concern has been with our own
divisions. (*Lambeth 1958,* SPCK, p. 1.29).

The Committee on Church Unity and the Church Universal
expanded this by stating:

We believe that the mission of the Church is nothing less than the
remaking and gathering together of the whole human race by
incorporation into Christ. In obedience to this mission we must
continually pray and work for the visible unity of all Christian
believers of all races and nations in a living Christian fellowship of
faith and sacrament, of love and prayer, witness and service.

The unity of the whole Church of Christ should be 'plain for
all men to see' (*ibid.* p.2.21).

The Conference was influenced by the work of Abbé Paul
Couturier and appealed for prayer 'for the unity of Christ's
people in the way he wills and by the means he chooses'
(*Resolution* 57, p.1.43).

In its Resolution on relations with the Methodist Church it
reiterated the statement of Lambeth 1948 that 'organic union'
should be

definitely accepted as the final goal, and that any plans for the
interim stage of intercommunion

should be

definitely linked with provisions for the steady growing together
of the Churches concerned. (*ibid.* p.1.38).

The 1968 Lambeth Conference met almost immediately after the Fourth Assembly of the World Council of Churches in Uppsala and in the wake of the Second Vatican Council. The committee on the Renewal of the Church in Unity endorsed the findings of the 1958 Conference, but added:

> We find ourselves impelled – but gladly impelled – to think first of the world. Its divisions clamour for healing and we see God's purpose for its unity as a cause even more urgent than the unity of the Church . . . Unity (of the Church) is desirable not only for its own sake but in order that the Church may be a better tool than at present in the service of God's purpose for the World. (*Lambeth 1968*, SPCK, p.120).

The Report then has a section on Christian Unity and Human Unity before setting out what it believes to be the 'Principles of the Anglican Quest for Union'. These principles begin with the unity of the Godhead and with God's gift of unity. 'Unity is inseparable from the renewal of the Church in holiness and truth and is always related to its mission'. The Church is called to be a 'foretaste of a redeemed creation, a sign of the coming unity of mankind'. (*ibid*. p. 122). They continue with a reiteration of and commentary upon the Lambeth Quadrilateral, offering the Anglican experience of a threehold ministry to be set alongside the experience of grace received through other forms of ministry including that of papal ministry (*ibid*. p. 124). This section concludes with an endorsement of the statement of the Third Assembly of the World Council of Churches at New Delhi on the nature of the unity we seek. The remainder of the Committee's report deals with issues of intercommunion in a divided Church and particularly with definitions of terms, with relations with particular Churches, and with the role and structures of the Anglican Communion.

Following the section on Relations with the Roman Catholic Church, that on Episcopacy, Collegiality and Papacy raises important issues. It is placed in the context of the conciliar character of the Church and of the *consensus fidelium*. Collegiality of the episcopate is seen to be particularly important in pointing to the worldwide and universal character of the Church 'at a time when most schemes for unity are being developed at a national level' (*ibid.* pp 137 f). In the search for worldwide unity the concept of primacy will need to be worked out in consultation with the Churches involved.

> We recognise the Papacy as a historic reality whose developing role requires deep reflection and joint study by all concerned for the unity of the whole body of Christ. (*ibid.* p.138).

The Resolutions of the 1968 Conference included the recommendation that a Permanent Joint Anglican-Roman Catholic Commission should be set up. They also complemented the concern with national and international unity affairs by giving priority to the search for unity at the local level. Each bishop was asked to apply the Lund dictum 'that we should do together everything which conscience does not compel us to do separately' to the working of his own diocese. 'Responsible experiment' was called for.

There were three meetings of the Anglican Consultative Council before the Lambeth Conference met again. At the Second Meeting in Dublin in 1973 the Report on Unity and Ecumenical Affairs notes the bewilderment felt by many at the failure of plans for united Churches to come to fruition, and the concentration upon local unity.

> There is indeed a sense in which it is right for Christians not to dwell upon the Church as an end in itself, as they pursue together those ends for which the Church exists in the worship of God, in the service of humanity, and in the spreading of the gospel. Yet it is necessary that the goal of actual Church union should emerge again as a powerful motive. The co-operation of Christians is now in a phase which cries out for intercommunion; but local intercommunion may lead to confusion and even sectarianism unless there are more than local approaches to the unifying of ministries and Churches There must be no shrinking from the conviction that, to use the New Delhi phrase, 'all in each place' should be one in ordered fellowship as well as in faith and sacrament. While avoiding any quest for uniformity or for centralisation, we reaffirm the conviction that organic union in the sense of united Churches is a goal for which intercommunion alone or federation alone is no substitute. *(Partners in Mission, ACC Dublin 1973,* SPCK, p.2).

In a paragraph entitled 'Full Communion' the Report suggests:

> that the term 'full communion' requires much more flexible application than has hitherto been the case. In the past it has been used with precise reference to interchangeability of ministers and communicants. But it is increasingly realised that to be in communion with another Church should involve much more spiritual sharing than that, and also that Churches can have a very real and also sacramental fellowship, while at the same time accepting certain limitations required by their own discipline. (*ibid.* p.6).

The Third Meeting of the ACC, held in Trinidad in 1976, heard from many parts of the Anglican Communion a questioning of 'the older model of organically united national Churches' (*ACC-3 Trinidad*, ACC 1976, p.14). 'National Church union schemes, in the opinion of some, tend to emphasise nationalism at a time when the Churches should be setting an example of unity which transcends national frontiers' (*ibid.* p.9). There was a search for 'new approaches and new models of visible unity at local, national and international levels' so that the unity of the Church might be seen 'as the sign and earnest of the unity of redeemed humankind' (*ibid.* p.15).

The Report attempts to summarise, with approval, recent thinking in the World Council of Churches. It focuses upon the New Delhi statement; upon the Uppsala idea that 'visible unity means diversified unity – the Church should be dynamically catholic, seeking diversity in unity and continuity, as a sign of hope of the coming unity of humankind'; and upon the concept of conciliar fellowship propounded at Salamanca in 1973 and Nairobi in 1975. It looks for new concepts and models of unity, and in particular sees visible unity as a dynamic process.

The 1978 Lambeth Conference devoted a great deal of time to the consideration of inter-Anglican unity, and this we have already noted. In its resolution on Ecumenical Relations it re-affirmed the readiness of the Anglican Communion . . . to 'work' for the time when a genuinely universal council may once more speak for all Christians;

it acknowledged:

the pressing need . . . that we should develop more truly sustained and sustaining relationships among the Churches as we look towards the time when we can enjoy full conciliar fellowship; (see *Breaking Barriers: Nairobi* 1975, p.60).

it encouraged the Churches of the Anglican Communion:

to pursue . . . the search for full communion and mutual recognition of ministries . . . on the basis of the Lambeth Quadrilateral;

and it called for a review of commitment to:

ecumenical structure *and* bilateral conversations at various levels with a view to strengthening the common advance by all Churches to the goal of visible unity. (*Lambeth 1978, CIO,* 1978 p. 48).

In its reference to relations with the Roman Catholic Church the Section on the Anglican Communion in the Worldwide Church commended the proposals of the Malta Report envisaging a process of advancing towards the goal of 'unity by stages' (*ibid.* p. 107).

In Resolution 30 the Conference took up the suggestion of ACC-3 and requested

the Anglican Consultative Council, in consultation with other Churches, to formulate appropriate definitions of terms used in inter-Church relations. (*ibid.* p. 49).

The section report from which this resolution was taken refers to:

the need for consistent terminology describing varying types and degrees of unity and definitions of ecclesial Communion

including such terms as 'organic union', 'conciliar fellowship', 'full communion', 'intercommunion', and 'restricted inter-communion' (*ibid.* p. 106).

This resolution was picked up, at least in part, by the Fourth Meeting of the Anglican Consultative Council in Ontario in 1979. This commissioned a study on the implications of 'full communion', and itself offered a distinction which could be made between Churches which actually define themselves by a relation of full communion with the see of Canterbury (i.e. Churches of the Anglican Communion) and those which do not so define themselves (e.g. the Old Catholic Churches or the United Churches of India, Pakistan and Bangladesh). (*ACC-4,* 1979, p. 14).

Professor Henry Chadwick was asked to produce an essay on this theme, which was eventually published in *The Churchman* (Vol.95, No 3, 1981, pp. 218–226), and a group produced a Study Paper entitled *Full Communion* for the ACC (ACC, 2189). The group themselves produced a summary of their argument as follows:

I.   The proper aim for separated Churches is ultimately *Organic Union.*

II. One stage on the way towards Organic Union is *Full Communion* between Churches. We wish to distinguish between

(a) *Full communion WITHIN the Anglican Communion,* and

(b) *Full communion WITH the Anglican Communion.*

On the way towards Organic Union, Full Communion is the appropriate stage in the case of Anglican relationships with episcopal Churches.

III. In the case of Anglican relationships with non-episcopal Churches an appropriate stage on the way towards Organic Union may be *Reciprocal Intercommunion.*

IV. We also offer some comments about *Other Forms of Intercommunion:*

(a) Official authorised 'Limited Admission' to the Holy Communion;

(b) The practice of Intercommunion by individuals or groups;

(c) Intercommunion as both *means* and *goal.*

The Fifth Meeting of the Anglican Consultative Council, held at Newcastle upon Tyne in 1981

took note of the Study Paper, but felt that its concentration on terminology excluded sufficient attention to the *implications* of full communion (*ACC-5,* 1981, p. 45).

Communion must be understood as involving more than *liturgical* celebration: it surely implies a visible sharing together in the common *life* of the Body of Christ. This seems to require some appropriate form of embodiment . . . the time is ripe for the consideration of some regional form of fellowship which would bring appropriate (episcopal) Churches together in common counsel and exchange (*ibid.* p. 46).

The Fifth Meeting of the Council also produced an interesting section on Unity – regional and universal. The entry of the Roman Catholic Church into the ecumenical scene and the WCC concept of conciliar fellowship now complement earlier models of a more local (national or regional) organisational unity.

Current interest focuses on Anglican identity, how to retain and indeed share it, without making it a ground of exclusion . . . the search for models of unity in which identity can be preserved and shared continues. A mere confessional federalism in which identity remains exclusive is seen to be inadequate . . . We therefore draw attention to the tension between international and more regional conversations and suggest that the underlying models of unity behind them should be examined (*ibid.* p. 45).

In preparation for the Sixth Meeting of the Council in Lagos in 1984 the ACC published *Steps Towards Unity*. This was published by the ACC in a second edition in 1984 including extracts from the proceedings of ACC-6. This document is still available and will not be considered here. However, to complete our historical survey we add a brief consideration of ACC-6 itself, which returned to the meaning and implications of full communion.

While not wishing to offer a complete and final definition of full communion, the term surely implies at least that the ministry of one Church or Province is in fact accepted by another, except in individual cases on individual and personal grounds – thus excluding the unacceptability of whole categories within the ministry of a particular Church. This applies both to the few remaining non-episcopally ordained presbyters of the Church of South India and to women ordained to the priesthood in the Anglican Communion when visiting Provinces which do not so ordain.

Full Communion surely also at least implies that there is some organ of regular mutual consultation between Churches if the communion between them is indeed to be a fellowship in life and mission as well as worship. (*Bonds of Affection, Proceedings of ACC-6,* 1984, pp. 91 and 92).

The Meeting made an interesting distinction between the final unity of the Kingdom of God and the fullness of unity which the Church should enjoy and express:

> In fact a variety of terms are currently in use for the fullness of unity – which will still fall short of the final unity of God with all his children – but which will nevertheless be a sign of reconciliation and of the Kingdom. Visible unity, full communion and organic union have all been used and each carries its own emphasis. They can mean different things for other Christian traditions and in the various dialogues with other Churches. (*ibid.* p. 91).

Hidden beneath these words is the fear that participants in the different bilateral dialogues in which Anglicans are involved may in fact be working with different models of unity and may even be working towards different short-term goals. In itself this would be understandable and perhaps acceptable. However it would be wrong if the different dialogues were found to be working towards goals which might ultimately prove to be incompatible.

A Provisional Examination of Terms

THE KINGDOM OF GOD

Even in a provisional consideration of the meaning of terms we should not lose sight of the fact that *the ultimate goal* of unity is the Kingdom of God, the city which comes down from heaven. It is called a kingdom because God's will is done in it. It is called a city because the inter-relationship of the citizens in love and justice has a form and structure. The fellowship, commonwealth or communion (*koinonia*), of which the Church is a sign, instrument and first fruits, is the salvation of humanity and the whole of creation redeemed in the Body of Christ. All the divisions of this age which damage wholeness of life, whereby one group dominates and oppresses another (rich and poor, slave and free, black and white, men and women), are overcome, while all the diversities of gifts which enrich life are retained. Ecumenism finds its proper context and motivation when God's mission of reconciling humanity to himself is top of the Church's agenda.

ORGANIC UNITY OR UNION

Organic union has consistently been a term used in Lambeth Conferences and in the Anglican Consultative Council to describe the goal of Christian unity. 'We believe that the Organic Union of all Christians and all Churches in each place, and of each place with every other, is the will of Christ' *(Full Communion: a Study Paper for the Anglican Consultative Council,* (2189) ACC, 1981, p. 3).

The same study paper goes on to quote a Church of England report:

> For separated Churches in the same area, the *organic union* of all in each place is the proper aim, because the visible and corporate unity of the local Church should be the embodied sign amongst men of the reconciling power of the love of God. God's Church is one, as God is one. This oneness is God's gift to those who obey the Gospel. It finds its proper expression when all the Christians of a locality appear as a single visible fellowship united in truth and holiness, displayed in love, service and worship (especially at the Lord's Supper) and active in evangelism. (*Intercommunion Today, being the Report of the Archbishop's Commission on Intercommunion,* p. 18, para. 30. England, 1968)

In Anglican and World Council of Churches' circles the term 'organic union' has normally been applied to the local, national or regional scene. Among all the reports of meetings of the Lambeth Conference and Anglican Consultative Council only one seems to have hesitations about organic union being the goal of unity. That was the Trinidad Meeting of the ACC, and one of the hesitations expressed was that the phrase had usually been used of *national* unions, and that the time had come when the Churches ought to be stressing *universal* unity (*ACC-3 Trinidad,* p. 14).

The Anglican Communion has eschewed any central organs carrying more than advisory status. 'Organic Union' has been a proper description of diocesan unity, where the bishop is a sign and instrument of unity alongside others. It has even been true of national Churches and of Provinces, which have been bound together by the collegiality of the bishops and in synods. Anglicans, however, until now have been careful not to give official conciliar status to the Lambeth Conference, not to regard the Anglican Consultative Council as a synod, and not to give the Archbishop of Canterbury any primacy except that of honour. It has not therefore used the phrase organic union to describe the unity of the Anglican Communion as a universal body. This is significant, because it has from the start used the phrase to describe its vision of unity. This raises the question of appropriate supra-provincial and supra-national organs of unity.

The phrase 'organic union' is taken from St Paul's image of the Church as the Body of Christ. It refers to the living, complementary and harmonious inter-relationship of the parts of the Church, each fulfilling a different function in order to enable the Church as a whole to live and act. Organic union therefore implies complex elements of organisation and harmony, and not merely a mechanistic centralisation. In the Church it implies a unity of faith which has scope for diverse expression, a unity of order in which various members are inter-related and mutually dependent on one another's fulfilment of their proper functions. Organic unity can most clearly be seen in a local Church where the Gospel is preached and the sacraments duly administered within the tradition, and where the bishop is a sign of unity and continuity with the past, the future and with Churches in other places. It can be seen in a Province where the bishops form a college, and bishops, presbyters and laity form a synod with powers to make appropriate decisions for the whole Province. It could be seen at a universal geographical level, were there a universal council having a similar authority, and a universal primacy or seniority.

> There will also be a universal dimension of this (organic) union, offering a sign of hope for the unity of all humankind. (*Full communion: a Study Paper for the ACC,* 1981, p.3)

This sentence is reminiscent of Resolution 20 of Lambeth 1908:

All races and peoples, whatever their language or conditions, must be welded into one Body, and the organisation of different races living side by side into separate or independent Churches, on the basis of race or colour, is inconsistent with the vital and essential principle of the unity of Christ's Church.

FULL COMMUNION AND INTERCOMMUNION

Although since 1931 the terminology used to describe various degrees of inter-Church relationship has been inconsistent and confusing, the most common usage has been that advocated by the Lund Faith and Order Conference in 1952, whereby the term *full communion* has been kept to describe the close relation which exists between Churches of the same denominational or confessional family, such as the Churches of the Anglican Communion, and of the Orthodox, Lutheran, or Reformed 'families' of Churches; whereas the term *inter communion* has been used to describe varying degrees of relation between Churches of one communion with a Church or Churches of another. Thus, for example, various Provinces and Churches of the Anglican Communion enjoy unrestricted *communio in sacris* with the Old Catholic Churches. Such unrestricted *communio in sacris*, involving complete sacramental fellowship and the mutual recognition and acceptance of ministries, has been described as '*full inter communion*'. (*Lambeth 1958*, p.2.23).

Lambeth 1958 abolished the distinction between full communion and full intercommunion.

In effectively confining the meaning of full communion to full interchangeability of ministers and members, it failed to take adequate account of two other elements which characterised the relationship between Anglican Provinces:

(1)   They had a regular organ of consultation in the Lambeth Conference, which there was not between Anglicans and Old Catholics.

(2)   Anglicans abhorred in principle and attempted (fairly successfully) in practice to abolish or avoid all overlapping and competing jurisdictions and parallel episcopates. The Anglican-Old Catholic agreement of 1947 specifically approved of parallel episcopates and jurisdictions (*Lambeth 1948*, p. II.73), and therefore was described as

'intercommunion' or 'full intercommunion', not as 'full communion'. The recent attempts to improve relations between Anglican Provinces and Churches with which they are, in the post-1958 phrase, 'in full communion', is precisely directed towards establishing structures of regular consultation.

The phrase 'full communion' therefore underwent a reduction in meaning in Anglican circles in 1958, and also appears to have different emphases in the various international theological dialogues with different denominations. All seem to be agreed that it means:

(a)   sharing a common essential faith;

(b)   full interchangeability of ministry and membership, including the participation of bishops of one Church in the consecration of bishops in the other.

most agree:

(c)   that it should include regular organs of consultation and common action (*Intercommunion Today,* p. 17; *Full Communion,* ACC; *Anglican-Lutheran Relations,* LWF, Geneva, 1983 p.13; although this was not mentioned in the 1958 *Lambeth Conference Report* p. II.23f) which confined the meaning to *communion in sacris.*

There is evidence to suggest:

(d)   that successive Lambeth Conference Reports also imply the intention that as an ideal there should be only one Anglican episcopal jurisdiction in each area.

There may be cultural, historical, linguistic or missionary reasons which may make it pastorally desirable or even necessary for a while to establish overlapping episcopal jurisdictions in the same area. However, these should always work in close collegiality with one another, and should exist for the ultimate purpose of more effective mission to particular groups and for the establishment of a just and proper unity between all people within the one Church of Christ.

Here, however, we frankly recognise that full and perfect communion in one sense must await the final arrival of the Kingdom of God. The history of the Christian Church is littered with both temporary and more permanent partial or extensive impairment of communion. Even within the Anglican Communion itself communion has sometimes been less than perfect. However, despite the absence of a central juridical authority, the Anglican Communion has hitherto overcome all threats to the breaking of communion. A recent threat to the full expression of communion has been the disagreement within the Anglican Communion over the ordination of women. While there are ordained (women) presbyters in one Province who are not (on principle, and not merely for personal and pastoral reasons) allowed to officiate as such in another Province, then full communion is impaired. So far the Communion has held together under the stress of a situation which arises from a diversity of theological views and cultural situations. The Lambeth Conference in 1988 will be called upon to maintain and strengthen the cohesion of the Anglican family despite the tension of this less than perfect expression of communion. The refusal of one Province theologically to recognise some of the priests of another Province as priests would be a more serious threat to communion than their juridical refusal to allow them to exercise their priesthood within that particular Province.

NEITHER FEDERATION NOR UNIFORMITY

The language used to describe relationships between Churches and Provinces has not been consistent during the past 120 years, but has been developing with developing relationships. In 1867 the relationship between Anglican Provinces was described both as 'intercommunion' and as 'full communion', but the latter phrase eventually superseded the former. So right up until 1930 the Anglican Communion was sometimes described as a 'federation' of Churches. Nevertheless, already in 1920 the Lambeth bishops had rejected 'a vague federation' of Churches as being an inadequate goal of unity. They similarly rejected 'uniformity'.

CONCILIAR FELLOWSHIP

The phrase 'conciliar fellowship' is relatively new.

The one Church is to be envisioned as a conciliar fellowship of local Churches which are themselves truly united. In this conciliar fellowship each local Church possesses, in communion with the others, the fulness of catholicity, witnesses to the same apostolic faith and therefore recognises the others as belonging to the same Church of Christ and guided by the same Spirit. They are bound together because they have received the same Baptism, and share in the same Eucharist; they recognise each other's members and ministry. (*Breaking Barriers: Nairobi 1975*, WCC, p. 60 and *What Kind of Unity?*, WCC, 1974, p. 121).

However the basic concept that the phrase conciliar fellowship conveys is very old and familiar to Anglicans, and perhaps owes something to the Lambeth Quadrilateral.

As we have seen, 'fellowship' was the theme underlying the Lambeth Appeal of 1920, and is the theme underlying the ARCIC *Final Report*. We have also seen that Anglicans have always been ready to have recourse to a truly ecumenical council of the Church. Where Churches are united locally, nationally and Provincially in organic unity, it is reasonable to expect that they should be held together internationally, and indeed regionally, by meeting representatively in Councils.

However, the phrase 'conciliar fellowship' has most recently been used to describe not simply councils of national or Provincial Churches in full communion, but also a structure whereby confessional traditions can 'retain an identifiable life' (*Facing Unity*, LWF, Geneva, 1985, p.16). This appears to be a modification of the original idea of conciliar fellowship such as came to the Nairobi Assembly from Salamanca. It appears to be influenced by the concept of 'Unity in Reconciled Diversity'.

UNITY IN RECONCILED DIVERSITY

Again 'Unity in Reconciled Diversity' as a phrase is a very recent arrival, which has scarcely been formally noticed yet in Anglican documents. However, much of the concept it describes is strongly present as early as *Lambeth 1920*. Even a cursory reading of the *Appeal to All Christian People* will show that in no sense was its vision of organic unity or of a 'visible, united society' aiming at a rigid uniformity. On the contrary within this unity Christian Communions now separated from one another would retain much that has long been distinctive in their methods of worship and service. It is through a rich diversity of life and devotion that the unity of the whole fellowship will be fulfilled (*Lambeth 1920*, p. 28).

We do not ask that any one Communion should consent to be absorbed in another. We do ask that all should unite in a new and great endeavour . . . (*ibid.* p. 29).

The united Church might even have the freedom to express the faith in different ways.

It may even be necessary to the Church that men in it should hold and expound different opinions, in order that the Church as a whole should have the whole of truth . . . (*Lambeth 1930,* p. 30).

However, in their desire for diversity and abhorrence of uniformity the bishops do not seem to have considered exactly how the varying traditions would be maintained after union. What has been envisaged by most Anglicans is that these traditions would mingle naturally and that what was good would be preserved without any conscious attempt to preserve them in water-tight compartments. Anglicans see unity and continuity preserved through the four elements of the Lambeth Quadrilateral, including episcopal ministry.

Within an episcopal Church and area it is conceivable that differing traditions may continue side by side, so long as they all accept their union with the one bishop and share communion at his hands. Episcopal ministry should especially care to preserve unity in diversity.

This is why Anglicans have in the past abhorred overlapping jurisdictions and parallel episcopates. Would Anglicans be prepared to consider some continuing confessional elements and even organisation, so long as locally this was held together under one bishop, whose episcopal ministry was exercised in close collegiality with that of all other bishops?

Universal Conciliarity and Primacy

We have not tackled the issue of the nature of universal conciliarity and/or primacy. It is not only discussion with the

Orthodox and Roman Catholics that is forcing Anglicans to consider this. It is also the rapid growth of the Anglican Communion and challenges to its internal unity. Successive Lambeth Conferences have stoutly maintained their resistance to any central authority or legislative synod, in favour of a consultative body for the 'autonomous' and 'independent' Provinces of the Communion. Lambeth 1920, however, pointed to that 'Christian freedom which recognises the restraints of truth and love' (*Lambeth 1920*, p. 26). The Lambeth Conference is a 'fellowship in the Spirit' (*ibid*. p 14). Today the word 'inter-dependent' is beginning to replace the word 'independent'. The role of the Archbishop of Canterbury as 'the *(sic)* focus of unity, was emphasised in *Lambeth 1978* (p. 98). Anglicans approach this issue from the opposite end to that of many Roman Catholics, who since Vatican II have been searching to find ways of avoiding the dangers of over-centralisation.

Questions are now being voiced about the role of the Anglican Consultative Council – has it a conciliar role? – are Provinces willing to yield any of their autonomy to it? Questions are being raised about the inter-relationship of the Anglican Consultative Council, the Primates' Meeting, the Lambeth Conference, and the Archbishop of Canterbury. These are questions about the personal, collegial and communal exercise of ministry and oversight, and about structures of decision-making. These are not purely Anglican questions. They have vital importance also for the progress of the ecumenical movement and the role of the Anglican Communion within it.

2
Churches in Full Communion

Ever since the 1888 Lambeth Conference adopted the Chicago-Lambeth Quadrilateral as a basis for sacramental fellowship and for eventual reunion, the Anglican Communion has established relations of inter-communion with certain Churches which were recognised as fulfilling the requirements of the Quadrilateral. This relationship was established at various times and in different places with the Old Catholics (Union of Utrecht), the Mar Thoma Syrian Church of India and with the Philippine Independent Catholic Church. Gradually, over the years, and especially, after Lambeth 1958, the term 'inter-communion' or 'full inter-communion' was replaced by the term 'full communion'. Because these Churches were seen as having their own history and their own communal and collegial structures, the Anglican Communion did not go beyond the full inter-changeability of ministries and members as far as relations with these Churches were concerned.

The adoption of the Lambeth Quadrilateral as a basis for unity and the successive pronouncements of the Lambeth Conferences regarding the desirability of organic union between different Churches in each place, also led, quite naturally, to the emergence of several local schemes of Church union in which Anglicans were partners. In the end the schemes which came to fruition were those which had originated in the South Asian sub-continent. The united Churches, which emerged first in South India and then in North India, Pakistan and Bangladesh, and in which there is a strong Anglican element should not be treated in exactly the same way as Churches such as the Old Catholic. The united Churches, at the time of inauguration, had only the various histories of the communions from which they had sprung.

Nor had they structures for communal and collegial interaction at regional and international levels. Their exclusion or near-exclusion from the deliberations of the Anglican Communion has been a grievous loss to them as well as to the Anglican Communion as a whole. Their growing involvement in Anglican councils is to be welcomed though it is not as yet commensurate with their size, strategic significance or relation of full communion. Their presence at the ACC in numbers which reflect their size and the presence of all their diocesan bishops at the Lambeth Conference would be welcome developments indeed. Their presence at other international and regional consultations, particularly ecumenical consultations and bilateral dialogues, would provide their leadership with much needed experience at this level and would also bring their specific experience and insights to the discussions.

Since ACC-3 (Trinidad 1976) there has been an understandable emphasis on unity at the international level and on the role of the Anglican Communion as a whole in seeking such a unity. This is to be welcomed. It should not be seen, however, as an alternative to local and regional schemes of union but as complementary to them. Christians of Anglican tradition who have joined other Christians, in obedience to the Lambeth fathers and often at considerable risk to their own identity, in local and regional schemes of Church union should not be isolated from the world communions from which they have come. They can best be remembered by giving the Churches which have come into being as a result of their endeavour a place in Anglican councils.

The publication of the document *Ministry in a Uniting Church* by the Commission of the Covenanted Churches in Wales has raised in a fresh way the problem of the relation between the Anglican Communion and those United Churches which have an Anglican component. The Welsh document has been presented to the various Churches in Wales for approval. If all the concerned Churches have approved the present document, the Commission will proceed 'forthwith' to draft a Scheme of Union. Some in the Church in Wales have already expressed their anxiety (in a way reminiscent of the anxiety expressed by some Anglicans at the time of Church Union in North India and Pakistan) that its participation in such a scheme of union would jeopardise its place in the Anglican Communion. The Welsh scheme relies heavily and at several key points on the North India and Pakistan scheme and it is, therefore, probably safe to say that the Anglican Communion would agree to a relationship of full communion with the united Church in Wales and that they would not experience the difficulties which the Church of South India had to face at first, in its relationship with the Anglican Communion. If, however, the *present* attitude to North India and Pakistan is taken into account, then there certainly will be a diminution in representation. It is this which needs to be addressed urgently by the ACC both in the case of South India, North India, Pakistan and Bangladesh and also in the case of Wales, and of any other Churches which may participate in a future union scheme at a national or regional level.

The emergence of the Welsh proposals at this time has revealed a fundamental tension in Anglicanism. Recent definitions of Anglicanism in certain quarters have held that the Churches of the Anglican Communion are those which *define themselves* by a relation of full communion with Canterbury (*ACC-4,* 1979). The implication is that those Churches which *are* in full communion with Canterbury but which do not so define themselves are not Anglican. This means that whenever there is a scheme of union which is entirely in keeping with Anglican principles, it will be opposed by some not because it is a departure from Anglican doctrine or ecclesiology, nor even because it will impair full communion with Canterbury, but simply because it will diminish representation in Anglican councils and will result in a loss of identity. It will be obvious immediately that such a definition of Anglicanism is a disincentive to ecumenism generally and in particular discourages the emergence of such schemes as that in Wales.

There may be reasons, both good and bad to treat the Welsh case as special because of its proximity to England. This would be a mistake if taken in isolation from the status of other united Churches and would be treated by the Churches of South Asia as discrimination against them. The problem raised by the Welsh proposals should be turned into an opportunity to guarantee the full and continued membership of the United Churches in the Anglican Communion should they so desire. (They may also be, of course, full members of other Christian world communions from which the constituent Churches have come). Such an act would allay the fears of those who feel that Church union will result in a loss of identity. It would also halt the increasing impoverishment of the Anglican Communion caused by the absence of representatives from areas where Church union schemes have come into effect. It may be that, in the long run, the term 'Anglican Communion' is no longer appropriate for a fellowship which contains more and more united Churches. It is true also that it is necessary to develop organs of consultation with the other Churches with which the Anglican Communion is in full communion. It may be that in due course a conciliar structure based on the Lambeth Quadrilateral should emerge which would encompass the present-day Churches of the Anglican Communion, the United Churches and other Churches in full communion. Should such an international structure emerge, it should not be paralleled by other, narrower, international structures. That would be indeed a denial of unity and collegiality. The emergence of such a conciliar structure would mean that the universal aspect of Anglicanism is subsumed in it. This is entirely in agreement with the wishes of the 1930 Lambeth Conference and would be the natural outcome of the Anglican movement towards fuller catholicity. In the meanwhile, the Anglican Communion should become more inclusive by encouraging the greater participation of the united Churches in its deliberations.

3
The Anglican–Roman Catholic International Commission

The Final Report

1. HISTORY

In 1968 the Lambeth Conference gave approval to the 'Malta Report' of the Anglican Roman Catholic Joint Preparatory Commission. This had been set up in 1966 – after consultation with the Primates – when the Archbishop of Canterbury and Pope Paul VI agreed to the establishment of 'a serious dialogue which, founded on the Gospels and on the ancient common traditions, may lead to that unity in truth, for which Christ prayed'[1].

The Malta Report proposed the establishment of the Anglican–Roman Catholic International Commission and the subjects upon which it should seek agreement, namely the eucharist, the ordained ministry and authority. It also recommended a number of areas for immediate pastoral co-operation between the two Churches and established the principle of 'Unity by Stages' as the most hopeful way forward in Anglican Roman Catholic relations.

The new Commission met for the first time at the beginning of 1970 and included Anglican representatives from the Church of Ireland, which provided the Anglican Co-Chairman, the Archbishop of Dublin, the Most Revd Henry McAdoo; the Anglican Church of Australia; the Anglican Church of Canada; the Church of England; the Church of the Province of Southern Africa; and the Episcopal Church of the USA.

The International Commission published interim and provisional work in 1970 but it was the following year which saw the completion of the first 'Agreed Statement', *Eucharistic Doctrine* at Windsor in 1971. The 'Windsor Statement' was duly received by the second meeting of the Anglican Consultative Council in Dublin in 1973 at which it was welcomed and commended to the Churches of the Anglican Communion for study and response.

A second 'substantial agreement' was claimed by the Commission in 1973 at Canterbury entitled *Ministry and Ordination*.

In 1976 at Venice a third agreement was reached – this time not claimed to be complete or substantial – entitled *Authority in the Church*. The following year Archbishop Donald Coggan and Pope Paul VI jointly welcomed and commended the work of the Commission thus far and called for its evaluation 'through the procedures appropriate to our respective Communions'.[2]

The Lambeth Conference of 1978 carefully examined the three Agreed Statements and in them was able to recognise:

> A solid achievement, one in which we can recognise the faith of our Church, and hopes that they will provide a basis for sacramental sharing between our two Communions if and when the finished Statements are approved by the respective authorities.
>
> (Resolution 33.2)

In 1979 the Commission at Salisbury completed its *Elucidations* of the Agreed Statements on eucharist and ministry, in the light of criticism from both Churches.

At Windsor in 1981 the Commission completed a second statement of authority dealing with the particular problems raised for Anglicans by the definition of the universal primacy of the bishop of Rome at the First Vatican Council of 1870. An elucidation of the earlier authority statement was also published together with an important theological introduction to the whole of the work of ARCIC setting its three subjects in the framework of an ecclesiology of *koinonia* – communion. All the earlier statements together with the new unpublished agreements were then published as the *Final Report* at the beginning of 1982.

Before publication however the 1981 Newcastle meeting of the Anglican Consultative Council gave careful and detailed consideration to the question of the evaluation of the *Final Report*. It established this process by formally putting to the Provinces the question of ARCIC posed to both Communions:

> Whether the Agreed Statements on Eucharistic Doctrine, Ministry and Ordination, and Authority in the Church (I and II), together with Elucidations, are consonant in substance with the faith of Anglicans and whether the *Final Report* offers a sufficient basis for taking the next concrete step towards the reconciliation of our Churches grounded in agreement in faith.
>
> (Resolution 4)

The Council also said:

> The completion of the *Final Report* of the Anglican-Roman Catholic International Commission raises the question in a way which demands very careful consideration by the Anglican Communion as a whole. How is it possible for a Communion of autonomous Provincial Churches to come to a common acceptance of an ecumenical agreement? The Council is quite clear that the formal acceptance of any ecumenical agreement remains with the Provincial Synods of the Communion. But the question then arises as to how and where an overall consensus is to be discerned and pronounced. While meetings of this Council and of the Primates are able to observe and encourage the process of study and decision, we believe the Lambeth Conference will be best able to discern and pronounce a consensus.

The Council also authorised the establishment of a new International Commission even while the two Churches were evaluating the work of the old. In Canterbury on the eve of Pentecost 1982 the present Archbishop of Canterbury and Pope John Paul II expressed profound gratitude for the work of the first Commission and duly established its successor:

> The Anglican-Roman Catholic International Commission has now completed the task assigned to it with the publication of its *Final Report* and, as our two Communions proceed with the necessary evaluation, we join in thanking the members of the Commission

for their dedication, scholarship and integrity in a long and demanding task for love of Christ and the unity of his Church.

The completion of this Commission's work bids us to the next stage of our common pilgrimage in faith and hope towards the unity for which we long. We are agreed that it is now time to set up a new international Commission. Its task will be to continue the work already begun: to examine, especially in the light of our respective judgements on the *Final Report,* the outstanding doctrinal differences which still separate us, with a view towards their eventual resolution; to study all that hinders the mutual recognition of the ministries of our Communions; and to recommend what practical steps will be necessary when, on the basis of our unity in faith, we are able to proceed to the restoration of full communion. We are well aware that this new Commission's task will not be easy, but we are encouraged by our reliance on the grace of God and by all that we have seen of the power of that grace in the ecumenical movement of our time.[3]

The next meeting of the ACC, in Nigeria 1984, reiterated the request of the previous Council for Provinces to respond 'to the ARCIC *Final Report* for ACC-7 in preparation for the Lambeth 1988'. (Resolution 28 [a]). It also requested a further meeting of ecumenical officers before ACC-7 to begin the task of collating the response of the Provinces to ARCIC and other ecumenical dialogues (Resolution 28 [c]).

In January 1987 the new Commission published its first Agreed Statement: *Salvation and the Church.* This in part responds to Anglican requests for work on justification by faith, noted and endorsed by the ACC in 1981.[4]

The present work of ARCIC II will include the question of Anglican Orders (for the resolution of which agreement in faith on eucharist and ministry is an essential part) and the ordination of women to the priesthood, within the framework of an ecclesiology of *koinonia*.

2.   THE GOAL

The goal of the Anglican-Roman Catholic dialogue has always been understood to be full ecclesial communion and visible unity. Intercommunion between a federation of separate Churches has not been felt to do justice to the gospel imperative for unity. So ARCIC I has spoken of 'full visible communion'[5] and the 'goal of organic unity'[6] while the Malta Report – endorsed by Lambeth 1968 – spoke of 'the quest for the full, organic unity of our two Communions'[7] and the Common Declaration of Archbishop Michael Ramsey and Pope Paul VI in 1966 saw the goal as 'a restoration of complete communion of faith and sacramental life'.[8]

The Common Declarations of 1977 and 1982 spoke in similar terms.[9] But this must not be understood to mean that there is yet a clear picture of what such 'full communion' would entail. The shape and nature of the goal can only emerge as dialogue and reconciliation proceeds. As the Malta Report expressed it: 'We cannot envisage in detail what may be the issues and demands of the final stage in our quest for the full, organic unity of our two Communions'.[10]

But full communion or organic unity does not necessarily imply organisational unity – though it does suggest the unity of an organism and of organic growth. Such a unity would be of relationship rather than identity.

> ARCIC I takes up the idea of unity in diversity when it says:
> The purpose of the universal primate's jurisdiction is to enable him to further catholicity as well as unity and to foster and draw together the riches of the diverse traditions of the Churches . . . Anglicans are entitled to assurance that acknowledgement of the universal primacy of the bishop of Rome would not involve the suppression of theological, liturgical and other traditions which they value or the imposition of wholly alien traditions.[11]

Furthermore, the basic ecclesiology of the *Final Report* – an ecclesiology of communion – presupposes that the fulness of the Church of Christ is to be found in the local Church and that the universal Church is not a pyramidically structured monolith but a diverse *communion* of local Churches.[12]

It must also be said that whilst intercommunion without commitment to fuller unity is an inadequate goal of Christian unity, this does not mean that some degree of sacramental sharing is inappropriate as a step or stage along the way to fuller communion such as was proposed in the Malta Report. We would expect and encourage ARCIC II to continue to work on the theological and ecclesiological basis for 'unity in diversity' and 'unity by stages' in the light of the increasing communion of faith we have and are coming to share and the increasing experience of real unity at the local level.

3. METHODOLOGY

The method of ARCIC I has not been to compare the conflicting – or at least contrasting – sixteenth-century formulas of our two Churches. The Commission has eschewed the juxtaposition of statements framed in an era of slogan and polemic.

This is set out by ARCIC in the following terms:

> In our three Agreed Statements we have endeavoured to get behind the opposed and entrenched positions of past controversies. We have often deliberately avoided the vocabulary of past polemics, not with any intention of evading the real difficulties that provoked them, but because the emotive associations of such language have often obscured the truth.[13]

Pope John Paul II, speaking to ARCIC I in 1980, eloquently summarised its method with apparent approval:

> Your method has been to go behind the habit of thought and expression born and nourished in enmity and controversy, to scrutinise together the great and common treasure, to clothe it in a language at once traditional and expressive of the insights of an age which no longer glories in strife but seeks to come together in listening to the quiet voice of the Spirit.[14]

This has meant that neither Church necessarily finds its usual denominational designations or terms within the agreed texts. Nevertheless the Commission believes each Church can recognise its own faith within the Agreed Statements.

The Commission has spoken of 'substantial' agreement on the eucharist and the ordained ministry. By this it has not claimed complete or comprehensive agreement but an agreement on the theological substance of the issues concerned which still allows for differences of theological emphasis, and pastoral or devotional practice.[15]

Speaking of different judgements about the propriety of eucharistic reservation and adoration the Commission illustrates its use of the term 'substantial agreement':

That there can be a divergence in matters of practice and in theological judgements relating to them, without destroying a common eucharistic faith, illustrates what we mean by *substantial* agreement. Differences of theology and practice may well coexist with a real consensus on the essentials of eucharistic faith – as in fact they do within each of our communions.[16]

It is important to note that such substantial agreement is *not* claimed for the texts on authority. Here convergence is more appropriate than consensus. In *Authority in the Church I* the Commission as a whole was agreed that a balance was required between:

'primatial' and 'conciliar' aspects of *episcope* serving the *koinonia* of the Churches . . . at the universal level.[17]

But the Anglicans went on to note their special difficulties with the definition of the Roman Primacy by the First Vatican Council. In its second statement on authority ARCIC I proceeded to examine these claims in detail. While possible ways of mutual understanding and agreement were charted the Anglican members of the Commission continued to reserve their judgement about the final authority of statements by a universal Primate unless they were received by the whole People of God. Thus the character of ARCIC's agreement on authority has a different quality from that of its agreement on the eucharist and ministry. There is also the important distinction between the eucharist and ministry, which are experienced within Anglicanism, and a jurisdictional universal primacy, which is not. Essential to a sympathetic understanding of ARCIC's approach to authority is the distinction the Commission itself makes between the actual state of the Church and 'the ideal of the Church as willed by Christ. History shows how the Church has often failed to achieve this ideal'.[18]

Thus the Episcopal Church in the USA accurately described the authority statement as a 'model of convergence'. The problem has to be faced in any ecclesiology, but becomes acute when Churches without certain structures of authority (such as episcopacy as well as universal primacy) are invited to accept them.

4.   RECEPTION AND RESPONSE

The response of the Provinces to the questions posed to them by the Anglican Consultative Council (for the Lambeth Conference 1988) must not be wholly identified with the wider reception of Anglican–Roman Catholic dialogue. Reception by the whole Church of an ecumenical agreement is a complex, profound and long term process which is as much concerned with local ecumenical relationships as the central decision making machinery of the Churches. Nevertheless the synodical responses by the Provinces are a visible instance of the wider process of reception which goes on before and after the formal synodical act. No structures of Church government can be identified without remainder with the *consensus fidelium* for the Holy Spirit can never be institutionalised. Nevertheless the formal synodical responses of the various Provinces of the Anglican Communion are an essential part of the wider process of reception.

To date (28th February 1987) 19 out of 29 Provinces have sent synodical (or official) responses to the Secretary General of the Anglican Consultative Council. They are:

(i)   The Anglican Church of Australia
(ii)   The Episcopal Church of Brazil
(iii)   The Anglican Church of Canada
(iv)   The Church of Ceylon
(v)   The Council of the Church in East Asia
(vi)   The Church of England
(vii)   The Church of the Province of the Indian Ocean
(viii) The Church of Ireland
(ix)   The Holy Catholic Church in Japan
(x)   The Church of the Province of Kenya
(xi)   The Church of the Province of Melanesia
(xii)   The Church of the Province of New Zealand
(xiii) The Church of the Province of Papua New Guinea
(xiv)   The Episcopal Church of Scotland
(xv)   The Church of the Province of Southern Africa
(xvi)   The Province of the Southern Cone
(xvii) The Church of the Province of Tanzania

(xviii)   The Episcopal Church of the USA
 (xix)   The Church in Wales

Most Provinces commissioned an appropriate theological committee to examine the *Final Report* in the light of the questions sent to the Provinces: that is whether or not the ARCIC I agreed texts are 'consonant in substance with the faith of Anglicans' and whether they provide a 'sufficient basis' for the next step forward. So, for example, New Zealand asked its Commission on Doctrinal and Theological Questions to draw up a report. Other Provinces established special committees for the same purpose, for example Australia. Yet others referred the *Final Report* to their official ecumenical commissions, as in the USA and Wales. In some Provinces there was a referral to the dioceses – as in Canada, England and the USA. In yet others, such as Ireland, the Standing Committee of the Province was responsible for the drafting of a report. In other Provinces the work of local joint Anglican–Roman Catholic commissions has been taken into account. In yet others one bishop or other theologian has introduced a debate in the Provincial Synod or the House of Bishops. These wide variations reflect the very different situations of the various Provinces. Not all Provinces have the administrative resources available for the compilation of a report on a complex set of theological texts when English is not the first language of the local Church.[19] Nor are Anglican–Roman Catholic relations on the same footing in all parts of the world. Some Provinces have therefore given a higher priority to debating the *Final Report* than others. The nature of a Provincial response has also been affected by the local ecumenical climate.

A distinction must also be drawn between what a Synod, Convention or House of Bishops, has actually said in formal resolution and the more detailed and discursive comments to be found in the Provincial Reports prepared as background for debate. While the resolutions passed by Synods must be interpreted in the light of the background reports prepared for debate it is in most cases only the resolutions which have the formal authority of the Province. It would therefore seem right to summarise first of all the resolutions of the Synods of the

Communion and then to look at the detailed reports for particular criticisms.

(i) *Australia*   The Synod of the Anglican Church of Australia (August 1985) simply endorsed the action of its Standing Committee in receiving the report of its special committee on ARCIC. It sent this Report to the Anglican Consultative Council as the Australian Response. The Report records divided views about ARCIC's treatment of eucharist and ministry. Some Australian Anglicans found the language of ARCIC on the eucharist 'went too far', others 'a very fair, if not exact representation of their own views'. The majority found the ministry statement 'a helpful, acceptable, scriptural and relevant affirmation of ministerial priesthood'. Less assent could be given to Authority. An Anglican pastoral primacy was preferred to the traditional Roman Catholic juridical understanding and the place of the laity in Anglican Synods was emphasised.

(ii) *Brazil*   The House of Bishops of the Episcopal Church of Brazil considered the report of its commission on ecumenical relations in March 1986. The Bishops had no adverse comments on the eucharist statement and were 'pleased with the agreement'. The Bishops also welcomed the ministry statement as in agreement with the ordinal of the Episcopal Church of Brazil in seeing the ordained ministry as a 'focus of leadership and unity of the diverse ministries of the Church'. They also praised ARCIC's understanding of ministry as service and the equilibrium of word and sacrament. They requested clarification of the representational role of the priest, asking whether priestly representation 'replaced Christ and his Church' or is the means 'by which Christ speaks and acts and the people take part in the one ministry of Christ'. The Bishops questioned whether discernment was only the prerogative of the clergy. With regard to authority, the Bishops concurred with the Church of New Zealand in resisting attempts 'to invest any organ of the Church with a teaching authority which is infallible'. But the Bishops went on to 'agree in

51

principle to the possibility of a universal primacy if exercised in a thoroughly conciliar manner with appropriate safeguards to prevent juridical control, and in collegial association with other orders of the Christian Church'. The Bishops asked for the positive experience of woman priests to be taken into consideration in the future, the question of the laity in Church government and election of Bishops.

(iii) *Canada* The General Synod of the Anglican Church of Canada (June 1986) was able to be more positive and passed resolutions stating that the ARCIC Statements on the eucharist and the ordained ministry were 'consonant in substance with the faith of the Anglican Church of Canada', that the texts on authority were 'sufficiently agreeable with Anglican teaching to provide grounds for continued dialogue', and that the *Final Report* as a whole provided 'a sufficient basis for the next concrete steps forward'. Canada had earlier endorsed the eucharist and ministry Agreed Statements and the debate in General Synod followed discussion and voting in diocesan Synods.

(iv) *Ceylon* The dioceses of Colombo and Kurunagala sent their responses to the Anglican Consultative Council in January 1987. The ARCIC *Final Report* had been jointly discussed in Sri Lanka by representatives of both Churches in a series of study programmes culminating in two residential sessions. The clergy of the two dioceses then met with lay advisors to formulate a response. While it was noted that the *Final Report* did 'not claim to present a comprehensive statement of the whole Catholic doctrine of the eucharist, ministry and ordination, and authority in the church, it nevertheless provided a basis for agreement between our two Churches while identifying the areas where further study and discussion were required'.

(v) *East Asia* The Bishops of the Council of the Church in East Asia (October 1985) sent the report of its Theological

Commission to the ACC 'as the work of the people in whose name it stands'. This sharply criticises the language, style and theological content of the *Final Report* as culturally inappropriate for Asia which is in an entirely different historical and political context from Europe.

(vi) *England* The Church of England General Synod meeting in November 1986, gave final approval to a series of resolutions on the *February Report*. This followed an earlier preliminary debate in July 1985 which preceded debate in all the Diocesan Synods. There had also been debates in the General Synod on the earlier publication of ARCIC statements. To assist the Church of England in its consideration of the *Final Report*, the Faith and Order Advisory Group of the General Synod had published *Towards a Church of England Response to BEM and ARCIC* and a *Supplementary Report* after the debates in the dioceses. The Resolutions passed by the Synod recognised both the eucharist and ministry texts of ARCIC I to be 'consonant in substance in the faith of the Church of England'. They were also recognised as providing the necessary basis for the reconciliation of the ministries of the two Churches. On authority the Synod went on to recognise 'sufficient convergence on the nature of authority in the Church for our two Communions together to explore further the structures of authority and the exercise of collegiality and primacy in the Church'. The Synod also affirmed the *Final Report* as offering a sufficient basis for the next concrete steps forward as listed in the Report of the Faith and Order Advisory Group. 'Following Motions' drew special attention to the need for further work on the role of the laity in the exercise of authority, the Marian Dogmas, and a universal primacy. Though all the resolutions were passed overwhelmingly in the House of Bishops, and substantially in the House of Clergy, there was a substantial lay minority with misgivings. Voting in the Diocesan Synods was more decisively in favour than at the General Synod.

(vii) *Indian Ocean* The Provincial Synod of the Church of the Province of the Indian Ocean met in Madagascar in September 1986 and debated the *Final Report* on the basis of a paper presented originally to the Seychelles Diocesan Synod by Archdeacon Charles James. This was forwarded to the ACC and commended by the Primate as expressing the view of the Provincial Synod. A Resolution was passed by the Synod 'accept(ing) the *Final Report* but with certain reservations in regard to the section on Authority'.

(viii) *Ireland* The Church of Ireland General Synod on 9 May 1986 declared itself unable 'realistically to answer with a general "yes"' the questions asked by the ACC on the grounds that they are 'so broad and relate to only part of what "agreement in faith" would have to entail'.

Interpreted in the light of the Standing Committee Report this appears to mean that there are other areas altogether which require consensus, as well as misgivings about some aspects of the *Final Report* itself. Justification by faith and Anglican Orders are then cited in the following resolution. A further resolution requests ARCIC II to consider the status of contemporary theology in relation to the official doctrine of the two Communions, the sacrifice of Christ and the Epistle to the Hebrews, and Scripture and Tradition.

(ix) *Japan* The House of Bishops of the Nippon Sei Ko Kei made its response to ARCIC *Final Report* in January 1987. The Japanese Bishops gave their 'positive acceptance of the work achieved' and said 'generally we subscribe to the statement and have little disagreement as to its theological treatment'. At the same time they felt the dialogue 'between the Churches has been centred too much on the European scene and mentality'. This was reflected in static western terminology such as 'irreformability' and 'infallibility'. They stress the important contribution to be made by the newer Churches of Africa and Asia and suggested that the larger number of non-European Bishops pointed to a review of the function of primacy and the 'inclusion of new elements'.

(x) *Kenya* The Church of the Province of Kenya has forwarded the preliminary response of its Provincial Board for Theological Education on the *Final Report* to the ACC (October 1986). This notes reservations about certain sections, giving as an example 'the concept of the Real Presence of Christ in the eucharistic elements, and the ambiguity of the word *anamnesis* (memorial)'. A further and fuller study of the *Final Report* has been commissioned.

(xi) *Melanesia* The House of Bishops of the Church of Melanesia commissioned a Report on ARCIC from its Doctrinal Commission. This was sent to the ACC by the Chairman of the Commission without enabling discussion by the House of Bishops. On the eucharist the Doctrinal Commission agreed that 'the statement is generally consonant with the faith because it expresses the biblical faith of the church and tradition which we teach and profess'. Similarly the ministry statement was judged to be 'biblically and theologically sound and in line with the tradition of the early Church'. It was however criticised sharply for not addressing the causes of division – especially *Apostolicae Curae*. The Commission only judged the first two sections of *Authority in the Church* to be consonant with Anglican faith. The Commission was critical of the 'common understanding of Roman Catholics' on the Petrine Texts, Divine Right and the Primacy of the Pope as 'essential for the nature and function of any *koinonia*'. These criticisms were not specifically directed at ARCIC.

(xii) *New Zealand* In July 1984 the General Synod of the Church of the Province of New Zealand received, endorsed and forwarded the report prepared by its Commission on Doctrinal and Theological Questions as its Provincial response to the *Final Report*. The Commission on Doctrinal and Theological Questions regarded the 'major part' of the statement on eucharist as agreement 'consonant in substance with the faith of Anglicans'. It regarded the admitted difficulties such as the range of meanings of *anamnesis* and the problem of a precise or generalised presence of Christ as resolvable on 'the principle of *lex orandi, lex credendi* . . . common worship and shared witness help to shape doctrinal consensus'. The Commission welcomed the work of ARCIC on ministry and said: 'We recognise in the document the faith of Anglicans'. On authority the Commission was 'willing to accept more than a 'primacy of honour' but '. . . wish(ed) to circumscribe any powers of jurisdiction very carefully'. It agreed 'in principle to the possibility of a universal primacy if exercised in a thoroughly conciliar manner with appropriate safeguards to prevent juridical control, and in collegial association with other orders of the Christian church'. It criticised the *Final Report* for insufficient attention to the actual role of the laity within Anglicanism.

(xiii) *Papua New Guinea*   The bishops of the Province of Papua New Guinea wrote to the ACC in May 1986 informing the Council that they had studied the *Final Report* of ARCIC and had discussed it with other members of the Church. They recorded 'complete agreement with statements on Eucharistic Doctrine and on Ministry and Ordination, accepting them as an accurate reflection of the faith of the Anglican position'. They went on to acknowledge that a universal primacy 'must involve a degree of jurisdiction' but hoped 'to see the legitimate rights and customs of local churches safeguarded within the wider framework of unity'. The bishops asked for guidance on whether one Province of the Anglican Communion could enter into a closer relationship with the Roman Catholic Church ahead of others.

(xiv) *Scotland*   At its General Synod of June 1985 the Scottish Episcopal Church recognised 'that the agreement on Eucharistic Doctrine in the ARCIC *Final Report* does not conflict with the tradition of the Scottish Episcopal Church'. The work of ARCIC on ministry was similarly accepted. Each section of the authority agreements was then examined and found to be acceptable as far as it went. A code of practice was requested concerning a shared universal episcopal jurisdiction and the Episcopal Church sought a 'restatement of Papal

Infallibility in terms of the guidance of the Holy Spirit'. The Synod finally listed and endorsed specific areas of pastoral collaboration.

(xv) *Southern Cone* The Province of the Southern Cone of America Theological Committee drafted a response to the *Final Report* which was then approved by the Provincial Executive Committee in November 1986. The Provincial assessment concluded that the Introduction (*Koinoinia*) was consonant in substance with the faith of Anglicans at the level of fundamental principles, though doubts remained at the level of specific doctrines. The statement on *Eucharistic Doctrine* was found to be consonant both at the level of fundamental principles and specific doctrines; the elucidation at the level of fundamental principles. Both agreed statements on *Ministry* and *Ordination* were held to be consistent with the current Anglican doctrine and practice at both the level of fundamental principles and specific doctrines. This approval was not however to be seen as a rejection of those churches which had not retained the traditional three-fold ministry. On authority the Southern Cone accepted the *Final Report's* handling of Scripture and Tradition, Councils and Reception (both at the level of fundamental principles and specific doctrines). It gave a more tentative acceptance to general jurisdiction and rejected ARCIC's conception of a Universal Primate. The Province preferred the concept of 'indefectibility' to 'infallibility'. It went on to suggest a new understanding of a more widely representative universal primacy. Such a primate would 'not be infallible nor enjoy immediate jurisdiction or authority . . . independently of the provincial structures'. Nor would the universal primate be necessarily linked to a specific see.

(xvi) *Southern Africa* The Church of the Province of Southern Africa asked the Southern African Anglican Theological Commission to prepare a study document and response to the *Final Report* in 1982. This was debated alongside the *Final Report* in the dioceses. At the Provincial Synod of July 1985 it was resolved *(nem con)* that the ARCIC texts on eucharist, ministry and authority 'are consonant in substance with the faith of Anglicans, and that the ARCIC *Final Report* does offer a sufficient basis for taking the next concrete step towards the reconciliation of our Churches grounded in agreement in faith'.

(xvii) *Tanzania* A report from the Provincial Synod of the Church of the Province of Tanzania was received by the ACC in February 1987. The Synod found 'the statements on the Eucharist and the ministry have treated in detail most areas of agreement'. It noted, however, that there were still some points of ambiguity about the eucharist. On ministry the Synod stressed the importance of an early resolution of the question of Anglican Orders. The Synod was less satisfied with authority. It stressed that Anglican forms of authority had been responsive to the varied cultural settings of the Churches and that the form of unity to be sought cannot yet be prescribed. It left open the question whether a Petrine Office for the service of unity in life and faith was a gift 'which God has already given to his people'.

(xviii) *United States of America* The General Convention of the Episcopal Church of the USA had already in 1979 resolved that the ARCIC Agreed Statements on Eucharist and Ministry 'provide a statement of the faith of this Church . . . and form a basis upon which to proceed in furthering the growth towards unity'. The Standing Commission on Ecumenical Relations therefore concentrated mainly on questions of authority in its detailed report to the 1985 General Convention. Among issues raised of particular importance were the overall question of the nature of authority itself, the role of the laity in the decision making processes of the Church and the problem of universal jurisdiction. The General Convention finally affirmed that the ARCIC handling of authority 'represents a theological model of convergence towards which both our Churches may grow and, in that sense, is sufficiently consonant in substance with the faith of this Church to justify further conversations and to offer a basis for taking further steps towards the reconciliation of our Churches'. It referred the Report of its Commission on Ecumenical Relations to ARCIC II.

(xix) *Wales* The Governing Body of the Church in Wales debated ARCIC in April 1985 on the basis of reports from its Doctrinal Commission and its Unity Committee. Resolutions were passed *nem con* accepting the ARCIC texts on eucharist and ministry as 'consonant in substance with the faith of the Church in Wales'. The authority texts were accepted by an overwhelming majority as recording 'sufficient convergence on the nature of authority in the Church' for further exploration of the structures of authority, collegiality and primacy. It was also agreed that the *Final Report* provided a sufficient basis for the next steps forward with particular attention drawn to the reconciliation of ministries, the exploration of a Uniate relationship and whether the Marian Dogmas would be obligatory.

5.   PARTICULAR QUESTIONS

(i)   *Eucharistic Doctrine*

(a)   Not all Provinces have been confident that ARCIC I's use of the word *anamnesis* (memorial) – although similarly used in *Baptism, Eucharist and Ministry* – resolves the problem of the relation of Christ's once-for-all sacrifice to the eucharist. New Zealand, for example, first acknowledges 'that ARCIC has firmly stated the fact that Christ's sacrifice on the cross is unique and unrepeatable' adding that 'the elucidation helps to clarify the lack of precision in the original statement', but then expresses its anxiety in the following way: 'Part of the problem stems from the very word *anamnesis,* which, because it can have varied theological tendencies, can cover to some degree the existence of opposed views of the Eucharist'.[20] ARCIC's speaking of the Church, through the Spirit, entering 'into the movement of (Christ's) self offering' has been widely coupled to the anxiety over *anamnesis.* The Church of England also registered this unease but went on to address it in the light of the different eucharistic theologies traditionally found amongst Anglicans both in the past and today.

> We understand that the words of the Windsor Statement and the elucidation imply a solidarity of Christ with his Church . . . whereby in our whole Christian Life we participate in his self-offering to the Father, sacramentally expressed in the eucharist. This implication is to be welcomed. It stresses that we can make no offering of ourselves (nor even make intercession) apart from Christ, with whom we have been made one in baptism, and who is himself the sole cause of our new standing with God . . .
>
> Beyond this there are differences of emphasis among Anglicans. On the one hand some stress our offering of ourselves in terms of grateful response to the once-made vicarious sacrifice of Calvary. They do not thereby exclude participation in the sacrifice of Christ (I Cor 10.16), nor do they exclude the intercessory aspect of the eucharist as entreating the merits of Christ's passion on behalf of the whole Church. Others, on the other hand, stress that our offering is possible because it is one with Christ's offering, and understand the eucharist to mean that sacramentally Christ offers himself in his people. The latter do not understand the act of offering as independent of Christ's . . . In both emphases the eucharist is both a thanksgiving for Christ's redemptive sacrifice, and a pleading of the Lamb of God who takes away the sin of the world.[21]

The New Zealand response also points to an eirenic solution in the *Baptism, Eucharist and Ministry* text (Eucharist 8 and commentary) and in Anglican liturgical formulas which speak of 'celebrating the memorial of our redemption' and 'our sacrifice of praise and thanksgiving'.

(b)   Several Provinces also record some anxiety about whether a receptionist understanding of the eucharistic presence is allowed for in the ARCIC statements. New Zealand puts it this way: 'Many Anglicans would still say with Richard Hooker, "the real presence of Christ's most blessed body and blood is not therefore to be sought for in the sacrament, but in the worthy receiver of the sacrament" '.[22] But New Zealand goes on to examine the *whole* of Hooker's treatment of this subject (Laws of Ecclesiastical Polity VI xvii) and makes clear that

Christ is not made present by the faith of the receiver. Hooker's Anglican 'receptionism' is a way of stating the gift of Christ's presence in the Eucharist, while declining an over-localised understanding of that presence. ARCIC is praised for moving towards 'a similar kind of reticence'.

The Southern African Theological Commission also raises this issue:

> One focus of differing balance and emphasis which continues to this day is found in the fact that some traditions place special emphasis on Christ's presence in the consecrated elements while others emphasise the presence of Christ in the heart of the believer through reception by faith. The report points out that acute difficulties arise when one or other of these emphases become exclusive. The Report has important things to say about this in section 7 of the elucidation – 'Gift and Reception'. 'In the opinion of the Commission neither emphasis is incompatible with eucharistic faith, provided that the complementary movement emphasised by the other position is not denied.' We believe that this is the correct position to take and that it accords fully with the Anglican tradition as found in the S.A.P.B. words of invitation 'Draw near and receive the Body and Blood of Our Lord Jesus Christ, which were given to you, feed on him in your hearts by faith with thanksgiving'; words which admirably epitomise the teaching of the Book of Common Prayer, Articles and Catechism on this subject. [23]

The Theological Commission urges Anglicans 'to be true to this formulary, regardless of which side of it they feel drawn to emphasise' so that 'the way forward will be not only clearer but more charitably trodden'.

(c) Issues relating to the reservation of the Blessed Sacrament were raised by a few Provinces. Ireland noted that 'veneration' of the consecrated elements created difficulties for some Anglicans. [24] The Southern Cone found this a difficulty in a Latin American context of 'popular Catholicism'. [25] Scotland, on the contrary, noted the long existing custom of the reservation of the sacrament in the Scottish Episcopal Church and spoke of reservation for the sick and those not able to be present at the celebration of the eucharist as 'one of the practices (with its associated devotional and doctrinal attitude

of reverence for the presence of Christ in the Bread and Wine
beyond the end of the service) which illustrate continuity with
the pre-Reformation Scottish Church'.[26] Wales and England
also welcomed ARCIC's eirenic treatment of reservation and
veneration when understood as an extension of the eucharist
itself. Ceylon expresses 'complete agreement with the Roman
Catholic Church on the fundamental question of the nature of
the Eucharist as a Sacrament actualising in time and space the
one sacrifice of Christ' and goes on to stress the importance of
maintaining 'that the sacrament is reserved for use when
necessary'. Agreement was recorded 'on the real presence of
Christ in the Eucharist though the forms and degree of
veneration may vary'.[24]

(ii) *Ministry and Ordination*
(a)   There has been widespread criticism of the lack of clarity
in ARCIC's description of the relation between the ordained
ministry and the priesthood of the whole people of God. This
has centred upon the assertion that the ministry of the ordained
'is not an extension of the common Christian priesthood but
belongs to another realm of the gifts of the Spirit'. Behind this
lies the unease of some Anglicans, for example in the Province
of the Southern Cone, at the sacerdotal associations of the
word 'priest' in spite of its official use among the Churches of
the Communion.[28] The Church of Ireland Standing Committee argues in favour of a 'representative' rather than a sacerdotal
priesthood:

> Because of Anglican comprehensiveness, which allows consider-
> able diversity of opinion among individual members of the
> Church, we cannot claim that the sacerdotal concept of ministry is
> *totally* rejected in Anglicanism. In the Church of Ireland, however,
> the presbyteral view of priesthood has normally been used over the
> years – a view which has for many generations been vigorously
> expressed by Anglican theologians.

The Church in Wales Doctrinal Commission posed the
problem in the following way:

> Is the ordained minister's authority independent of the Church or is
> it derived from the Church? The precise relationship between the
> priesthood of the whole people of God to the ordained ministry is

therefore unclear in the Statement and whereas we may agree that the ordained minister is set apart in some sense, the differentia of this minstry needs to be examined more carefully.

Though remaining critical of the ARCIC phraseology the Church in Wales Provincial Unity Committee was more positive, recognising that the ordained ministry was distinctive and accepting that 'it is appropriate to refer to it as "priestly" '.[29]

Similarly the Church of England Supplementary Report, while criticising the original text of the ARCIC statement, makes a careful Anglican defence of the priestly quality of the ordained ministry.

> The ordained ministry speaks and acts in the name of the whole community. It also speaks and acts in the name of Christ in relation to the community. Its authority and function are therefore not to be understood as simply delegated to it by the community. Consequently, in so far as its ministry is priestly, its priesthood is not simply derived from the priestliness of the whole community. Rather, the common priesthood of the community and the special priesthood of the ordained ministry are both derived from the priesthood of Christ. Bishops and presbyters do not participate to a greater degree in the priesthood of Christ; theirs is not an intensified form of the common priesthood; they participate in a different way – not only that is as individual believers, but in the exercise of their office.

(b)   Several Provinces drew urgent attention to the need for the reconciliation of ministries. Melanesia, for example, is critical of ARCIC for not addressing the problem of *Apostolicae Curae*. It calls on the Roman Catholic Church to 'revoke the statement of Pope Leo XIII which declares Anglican Orders null and void'.[30] The Irish response also vigorously rehearsed arguments for the unsoundness of Pope Leo's judgment and expressed the hope that 'some concrete results will follow (ARCIC II's) deliberations on this subject'.[31] Other Provinces, such as New Zealand, Scotland, the USA and Wales, look forward to the reconciliation of ministries as an essential part of the next stage towards fuller communion.

(c)   Both Canada and New Zealand, as well as some other Provinces raise the question of the ordination of women to the priesthood. Responses from the Canadian dioceses indicated that this was a priority:

> The fact that the Roman Catholic Church has said that it does not believe it possible to ordain women to the priesthood poses an obstacle to the reconciliation of ministries that must be urgently addressed.[32]

England noted the correspondence between the Archbishop of Canterbury and Cardinal Willebrands and that the matter was being taken up by ARCIC II.[33]

(iii) *Authority of the Church*

The responses of the three texts of ARCIC on authority reflect the sensitive nature of the issues under discussion and are of a different quality from those on eucharist and ministry. Whereas the eucharist and the three-fold ministry have been a constant feature of both Roman Catholic and Anglican experience, the rejection of the jurisdiction of the Bishop of Rome has been a distinguishing feature of Anglicanism. The statements on authority in effect ask the critical question whether being out of communion with the Roman see is an accidental and contingent fact of history or of the very substance of being an Anglican. For those who believe the latter ecumenical dialogue will necessarily be a threat to Anglican identity, and agreement between Anglicans and Roman Catholics will appear to them to be a contradiction in terms. Whatever hesitations and criticisms Provinces have recorded in relation to the statements on authority, there is little of such fear in their responses and much to suggest that representative Anglicans have begun to share something of the ecumenical vision expressed by the Scottish Episcopal Church:

> As Anglicans seek no longer to justify our existence in separation from the Pope, but rather to understand what the Papacy means in the life of the Roman Catholic Church and how the ministry of the Pope could strengthen the life and witness of the Anglican Churches, we ask the Roman Catholic Church to be willing to aid us patiently in this process of reappraisal of an office we have lived without for so long, and which has developed considerably during that period. We also ask the Roman Catholic Church so to foster the ecumenical vocation of the Bishop of Rome that the universal

pastorate of the Pope may begin to become an experienced reality within the Anglican Communion on our way to the fulness of unity, and without the precondition of subscription to Roman Catholic formulations of Papal authority in their entirety.[34]

To adopt such a spirit does not mean Provinces have been uncritical and a number list issues where serious problems remain to be resolved or questions continue to need elucidation by ARCIC II.

(a) Several Provinces speak of the need for a further elucidation of the relation of Scripture and its interpretation in the developing tradition of the Church. Discussion in some Provinces has revealed a continuing inter-Anglican debate in this area. As for example in England. In commending the Elucidation to Authority I the Faith and Order Advisory Group of the Church of England expounded the dynamic relation between Scripture and Tradition thus:

> On the one hand, Scripture comes from the living proclamation of the Church, and the formation of the Canon takes place within the experience of the Church's worship and is the product of it. On the other hand, the Church has always treated Holy Scripture as the criterion or norm for the post-apostolic Church; and the development in the interpretation of the original datum of divine revelation is a continuing process through which Tradition comes to be formed . . . Accordingly, while ARCIC plainly gives primacy to the Authority of Scripture, the Commission has not argued for Scripture being the sole and exclusive source of guidance . . . Although the Commission can hardly be held guilty, as they have been accused, of failing to give account of the primacy of Scripture, there still lie behind their reports questions about the authority and interpretation of Scripture, about the significance of the closing of the Canon, and about the dynamic nature of tradition. These are questions which in the future Anglicans and Roman Catholics will need to explore together.[35]

(b) Other Provinces have asked for a clearer distinction to be drawn between authority and power. The Episcopal Church of the USA, for example, observed that 'one needs only to point to Christ himself, who in his cross used no 'power to require compliance' but whose authority there reaches its highest expression'.[36]

(c)   Some Provinces have questioned the strength of the argument leading to a universal primacy exercised by the Bishop of Rome. The Welsh Unity Committee put it this way:

> The need for a universal expression 'of the general pattern of the complementary primatial and conciliar aspects of *episcope* serving the *koinonia* of the Churches' if 'God's will for the unity in love and truth of the whole Christian community is to be fulfilled' could perhaps be justified, but except on grounds of historical tradition and the claims of the Papacy in the past it is not self-evident that such a universal focus should be permanently located in Rome.[37]

The Southern Cone also questioned the Roman location for a universal primacy.

(d)   Almost all Provinces which have included a detailed response with their Synodical decisions have asked for further discussion of the relation between primacy and episcopal collegiality. As has been seen some Provinces included this in their acceptance of ARCIC I as a basis for further discussion. Speaking of the possibility of primatial interventions in the life of the local Church the USA Report says:

> Such interventions would have to be explicitly defined by binding agreements between our two Churches to ensure the 'moral limits' of its exercise

and

> If Anglicans grant the need for a universal primacy, as so eloquently argued in the *Final Report* 'as a sign and agency of catholic unity, some such system of restraints needs to be explored lest primacy be exercised heteronomously, to the detriment, rather than to the welfare of the Body of Christ.[38]

(e)   Similarly, there have been requests for further discussion of the relation between primacy and conciliarity. So the Australian Report looked rather to an Anglican pattern of authority:

> While recognising some sense of need for a greater primatial role than presently exercised in the Anglican Communion, it was felt that Anglican patterns of Primacy with its pastoral emphasis and limited authority, might be a pattern for other Churches to follow. The model of 'Bishop in Synod' offered ways of distribution and exercise of authority involving a wider and helpful participation.[39]

The Southern Cone also offered an alternative model of primacy based more on Anglican than Roman Catholic practice.

(f)   Related to this is the role of the laity in the decision making structure of Anglicanism. Further work on this important question was raised by a majority of Provinces and this perhaps constitutes the most serious and persistent criticism of ARCIC I's treatment of authority. The Episcopal Church in the USA acknowledged that according to the *Final Report*

> Laity *may* participate in councils. 'In all these councils, whether of bishops only, or of bishops, clergy and laity, decisions are authoritative when they express the common faith and mind of the Church'.[40]

But then goes on to note that the interest of the *Final Report* quickly moves to the special role of bishops in the defining of faith. The Episcopal Church recognised 'that this focus was inevitable at this stage of the dialogue' but insisted that a 'synodical structure has gradually commended itself throughout Anglicanism and should not be lost'. It concluded by pointing to:

> the increased attention currently being given to the ministry and vocation of the laity in both our Churches by reason of their baptism (and) urged careful consideration of this matter in future conversations.[41]

The general criticism of an inadequate account of the role of the laity in the Church was tempered by an awareness of its comparatively recent development in some Provinces, notably England. New Zealand acknowledged that:

> *theological reflection* on the Anglican Communion's experience (of Synodical government) is generally undeveloped, and diverse notions of Anglican 'comprehensiveness' mean that it is very difficult for any discussion to develop a consistent Anglican ecclesiology . . . we do, however, wish to point to a historical experience and a theological resource which seems to have been only superficially exploited by ARCIC.[42]

(g)   Several Provinces recorded an initial anxiety at ARCIC's treatment of ecumenical councils in *Authority in the Church I*. The language about councils was felt to be ambiguous and to be open to the implication of an automatic inerrancy in contradiction to Article 21. The discussion of 'reception' in the Elucidation of *Authority in the Church I* allayed much disquiet – Scotland, for example, valued highly ARCIC's clarification of the reception of councils – but the Episcopal Church in the USA also 'hoped to see the same criteria regarding reception applied to *both* papal and conciliar statements'.[43] So too did the Church of England:

> So while welcoming what the Commission says generally about reception of conciliar statements . . . we would agree with the Anglican members of the Commission that the papal statements ought no less to be subject to the same process of reception even when they are made after conciliar consultation. However, we note with gratitude the Commission's own judgement on this matter that 'contemporary discussions of conciliarity and primacy in both communions indicate that we are not dealing with positions destined to remain static'.[44]

(h)   Similarly, Provinces have posed questions about 'infallibility'. The Southern Cone reported:

> We agree that primates as well as councils have defended legitimate positions against attack and that authority ought to work in this way, but this does not guarantee that its decisions are always right. We doubt whether there is another way of checking whether the decisions taken are right or not apart from waiting for the process or reception by the members of the universal church to take place (AII 31). The final reference to the universal primate's task, 'he should have both a defined teaching responsibility and appropriate gifts of the Spirit to enable him to discharge it', (AII 33) leaves the question open.[45]

(i)   A particular instance of the problem of 'reception' in a divided church is the case of the two Marian definitions of the Roman Catholic Church. Several Provinces drew particular attention to this problem.

The Southern Cone said:

> ARCIC accepts that the Marian dogmas are a problem for many Anglicans and says that it should be specifically stated whether the recognition of papal primacy automatically implies subscription by Anglicans to both the dogmas of the Immaculate Conception and the Assumption of the Mother of our Lord.[46]

The USA noted that the problem concerns both the *content* of the definitions and their *authoritative status:*

> To pose this question is not to deny that some Anglicans believe the Marian dogmas already *as doctrines*. Further work can and should be done to render them as intelligible as possible to the Anglican communion as a whole. To restate these doctrines as possible *theologoumena* however, does not obviate the dogmatic issue. We would raise the question of the status of these dogmas in the hierarchy of truths recognised by the Roman Catholic Church.[47]

6. UNDERLYING QUESTIONS

(i) The Report prepared by the Standing Committee of the Church of Ireland insists that 'due cognisance of the official doctrines of our two communions' must be taken. After considering the text in some detail the Irish Report devotes a whole section of its consideration of the *Final Report* 'in relation to the Preamble and Declaration and the Articles of Religion of the Church of Ireland'. Other Provinces have only referred to the Articles where there has been a question of a possible contradiction. Some Provinces make no reference to the Articles at all as they are not part of their constitution or entailed in their declaration of assent. Ireland also comes to the judgement that there is 'a real divergence between contemporary Roman Catholic theologies and official Roman Catholic doctrine'.[48] In particular the theology of ARCIC's Agreed Statements is said to be at variance with the authoritative teaching of the Roman Catholic Church.[49] Other Provinces have not entered into the question of the compatibility of the *Final Report* with Roman Catholic faith. The Church of Ireland resolution requesting further consideration of the status of contemporary theology in relation to the official doctrines of the two communions appears to propose a different methodology from ARCIC I. A comparison of confessional formulas is envisaged rather than ARCIC's avowed aim of discovering contemporary agreement in faith (see above 3, Methodology).

Another difficulty arising in responses to the eucharist and ministry Statements has been that of different assessments within individual Provinces. This has been especially noticeable where differences of churchmanship persist. The Australian Committee 'sought to test (ARCIC's) Statements against the traditions which lie within the Anglican Communion'.[50] Other Provinces where there are strong differences of churchmanship approached the task in the light of the whole spectrum of the tradition of their Province rather than particular parts of that tradition. The Church of England in particular attempted to state a *common* Anglican conviction on both eucharistic sacrifice and the priesthood of the ordained ministry against which to test the compatibility of the ARCIC Statements with Anglican faith (see above 5 Particular Questions i.a and ii.a).

(ii)   Another matter of quite a different order is the question of the different 'context' of the *Final Report* and of some of the Provinces responding to it. This is stressed strongly by the Theological Commission of the Council of the Church of East Asia. The point is also made by the Holy Catholic Church of Japan. After speaking of being generally able to subscribe to the *Final Report* the Japanese House of Bishops continues:

> We recognise, of course, that there remain various issues requiring further attention. In particular, in the mind of many Anglicans there is a suspicion of the centralised power structure historically associated with the exercise of universal primacy. From a Japanese perspective, we might also ask how far the report does justice to the situations and insights both of other denominations and Christianity outside the European-North American cultural sphere. This said, however, we would stress that our basic response to the *Final Report* is a positive one, of thanksgiving, consensus, and hope for the future.[51]

A similar view is echoed by Ceylon.

The Province of the Southern Cone also stresses the importance of a contextual understanding of ecumenical dialogue (and its difficulties) in Latin America:

> We believe that theology is not an abstract science but one that always speaks to a specific community which has its own cultural heritage and which lives facing problems peculiar to its setting. Our Province is one of the few members of the Anglican Communion living in a totally Catholic environment. The type of

Roman Catholicism seen in these countries is very different from that found in Europe and North America and many parts of the world. The situation is well summed up in the words of a Peruvian author: 'The bulk of Catholics (in Latin America) do not profess that reflexive, intellectualised and critical religion which is proposed but the intuitive, disciplined, ritual faith which has always given strength to the Church among us: 'La fe del carbonero' (the Charcoal-burner's faith).[52]

The Report then goes on to describe some of the characteristics of Latin American Catholicism. It stresses the very differentiated nature of the Roman Catholic Church:

Structurally the Roman Catholic Church in our continent is one, but in practice we have before us several 'churches', with little unity among themselves, (sometimes even at the level of bishops).[53]

'Progressive' or 'charismatic' sectors of the Roman Catholic Church had shown much openness to ecumenism. The contextual nature of the Southern Cone response is illustrated by their objection to reservation of the sacrament and that ARCIC had not spoken of masses for the dead – both important in Latin American popular cultus. This was in spite of agreement with the 'fundamental principles' of both the original statement and its elucidation.

7. CONCLUSION

The preparation of this provisional collation and assessment of Provincial responses to ARCIC I by the Anglican Ecumenical Consultation of bishops and ecumenical officers must be seen in the wider context of the wider reception of ecumenical dialogues by the whole Church. This is a continuing process but its immediate sequel will be the Singapore meeting of the ACC and the Lambeth Conference of 1988 for which this report is prepared.

After the inspired beginnings of reconciliation between Anglicans and Roman Catholics during and immediately after the Second Vatican Council came the decision of the Lambeth Conference of 1968 which inaugurated the work of ARCIC I. Twenty years later we see the fruits of the labours of ARCIC and the work of the Churches in responding to it. We urge the Communion to see this work through to its conclusion – even though the present patient task of careful assessment and evaluation is necessarily less exciting than its beginnings. The continuing and ending of the task begun requires steadfastness and fidelity to the original vision given expression by Pope Paul VI and Archbishop Michael Ramsey in their quotation from St Paul's letter to the Philippians: 'Forgetting those things which are behind, and reaching forth unto those things which are before, I press towards the mark for the prize of the high calling of God in Christ Jesus.' (3.13-14).[54]

ACC-7 will therefore have the immediate task of continuing the evaluation of this dialogue by testing, amending and expanding this interim assessment in preparation for the Lambeth Conference of 1988. The ACC will be able to do this on the basis of its episcopal, presbyteral and lay membership and its representation from all the Provinces. We hope this continued reflection will stimulate and encourage an official response to the dialogue from Anglican Provinces which have not as yet been able to respond.

The ACC will need to consider how to help Provinces for whom this is difficult – such as the many which do not have English as their first language and those for whom the primarily western theological language of ARCIC I does not easily translate into the idiom of very different cultures. Particular problems arise over ecumenical agreements in some Provinces where key theological words – such as the word for God – have traditionally been translated differently by Protestants and Catholics. We commend the careful work begun in Japan where the study of ARCIC reports has been conducted simultaneously with joint Anglican–Roman Catholic translation of the texts.

We also commend to the Provinces the first Agreed Statement of ARCIC II, *Salvation and the Church*, for study, reflection and appropriate response. We believe this agreed text may assist many Anglicans to a more positive evaluation of the earlier *Final Report*, where there have been residual doubts about agreement in faith with the Roman Catholic Church on even more fundamental matters than the nature of the eucharist, the ordained ministry, and authority in the

Church: namely the theological ground of our new standing before God – justification by grace through faith. We also believe many Anglicans will be helped by this new Statement to see the quest for Anglican–Roman Catholic unity as complementary to other parts of the ecumenical pilgrimage. Agreement on justification by faith by Anglicans and Roman Catholics would have positive implications for Anglican relations with other Christian families which have experienced the Reformation. Along with *Baptism, Eucharist and Ministry* the agreement on *Salvation and the Church* by ARCIC II should give assurance to Anglicans that movement towards Anglican–Roman Catholic reconciliation is not movement away from Churches of the Protestant tradition. The ecumenical movement is one.

The process of reception for the Anglican–Roman Catholic dialogue will reach a significant moment at the 1988 Lambeth Conference. ACC-7 will need to continue the discussion begun at ACC-5 which believed 'the Lambeth Conference will be best able to discern and pronounce a consensus on the completed work of ARCIC I'. To discern and pronounce this 'common-mind' the bishops of the Lambeth Conference are being asked by the Anglican Consultative Council to do more than offer an opinion. Though there can be no question of a legislative or juridical decision, there are moments when the Lambeth Conferences have discerned, articulated and formed the common mind of the Anglican Communion on important matters of faith and morals. The bishops are being invited to listen and speak, to determine whether there is a recognisable and coherent path for the Communion in this matter. The bishops will take account of discussion in their own dioceses among priests and people, especially where Anglicans and Roman Catholics work and pray together. They will be informed by the Synodical decisions of their own Province. But in the end the bishops have a special responsibility for guarding and promoting the apostolic faith, a responsibility which is theirs by ordination and office. At Lambeth they will talk together in collegial association with their episcopal colleagues of the dioceses of the entire Anglican Communion and with the priests and laity of the Anglican Consultative Council meeting with them.

Even so this is only part of reception. Any canonically changed relationship consequent upon sufficient agreement in faith would rest with the Synodical authority of each Province. This process, combining local and worldwide elements, has a parallel on the Roman Catholic side as the Vatican has asked the various Episcopal Conferences throughout the world whether they can recognise their faith in the ARCIC *Final Report*. This is itself a development of some significance. Many of these Roman Catholic responses to ARCIC I have been highly positive, for example the published response of the Roman Catholic bishops of England and Wales. Although final evaluation will undoubtedly be made by the competent Roman authorities it is quite probable that any eventual changed relationship on the Roman Catholic side would still need to be implemented locally by the Episcopal Conference in ways appropriate to each country or region. Anglicans should welcome this exercise of the principle of subsidiarity and decentralisation.

As noted above, almost all Anglican Provinces which have so far responded have been able to recognise their faith in what ARCIC I has said about the eucharist and the ordained ministry. The bishops will need to ask themselves whether they – as bishops of the Anglican Communion – can say that, in spite of questions and limitations, the ARCIC I agreements on eucharist and ministry are consonant in substance with the faith of Anglicans. On authority ARCIC I does not claim complete agreement. The bishops will need to ask themselves whether they – as bishops of the Anglican Communion – can say that the agreements on authority are sufficiently in accord with Anglican teaching to provide the ground for continued dialogue on authority in the Church. In the light of the criticisms of the Provinces, such a continued dialogue would need to pay special attention to conciliarity and the Anglican synodical tradition, and to the collegiality of the whole episcopate and the exercise of primacy as a focus of unity in the universal Church.

In the meantime we encourage ARCIC II to continue its work on other issues which still impede a further growth in communion, namely the inability of the Roman Catholic Church to recognise officially the ordained ministry of the Churches of the Anglican Communion – whether by reason of Pope Leo's Bull *Apostolicae Curae* or the ordination of women to the priesthood in some Anglican Provinces. We are also glad that ARCIC II will examine how far perceived differences in teaching on moral issues will be a potential impediment to fuller communion. We note that tensions within the Roman Catholic Church in some countries are being received with sympathy and anxiety in their neighbouring Anglican Provinces. The relationship between the actual exercise of the existing Roman primacy and episcopal collegiality will no doubt be part of ARCIC II's continuing discussion of authority.

We welcome the intimation from ARCIC II that it hopes to set all this future work in the overall context of an ecclesiology of *koinonia* (communion, community or fellowship). We believe this is the proper biblical and patristic foundation for such discussion. We also believe the understanding of the Church as a communion to be the fruit of the contemporary experience of both our Churches as they continue to discover what it is to be 'the community of those reconciled with God and with each other because it is the community of those who believe in Jesus Christ and are justified through God's grace'. 'Only (such) a reconciled and reconciling community, faithful to its Lord, in which human divisions are being overcome, can speak with full integrity to an alienated, divided world, and so be a credible witness to God's saving action in Christ and a foretaste of God's Kingdom'.[55]

NOTES

[1] Common Declaration, 1966, *Final Report,* p. 118.
[2] Common Declaration, 1977, para. 4, *Final Report,* p. 120.
[3] Common Declaration, 1982 2 and 3, *Bonds of Affection,* ACC, 1984.
[4] Report of ACC 5, p. 40.
[5] *Final Report,* Introduction 9, p. 8.

[6]   *Final Report,* Conclusion, p. 99.
[7]   Malta Report 17, *Final Report,* p. 113.
[8]   *Final Report,* p. 118.
[9]   Cf *Final Report,* p. 121 and *Bonds of Affection,* p. 107.
[10] *Final Report,* p. 113.
[11] *Final Report,* pp. 90, 91.
[12] Cf *Final Report,* Introduction 6 and 7, pp 6-7.
[13] *Final Report,* pp. 66, cp also p. 1-2.
[14] Cited from *They are in Earnest,* Yarnold SJ, St Paul, p. 210.
[15] Cf Elucidation: Eucharistic Doctrine, para 2, *Final Report,* p. 17.
[16] *Final Report,* p. 24. For an elaboration of the meaning of 'substantial agreement' and other terms cf *Diversity and Communion,* Yves Congar, SCM Press, 1984, p. 140.
[17] *Final Report,* p. 64.
[18] *Final Report,* p. 50.
[19] This problem was recognised at ACC 6, where a resolution (28 (b)) called for consideration of how help could be given to Provinces in studying and assessing the ARCIC *Final Report* where English is not spoken as a first language.
[20] CPNZ Commission on Doctrine and Theological Questions: report to the General Synod on the *Final Report* of ARCIC B. 1. 3.
[21] *Towards a Church of England Response to BEM and ARCIC,* CHP, London 1985, paras 185 and 186.
[22] CPNZ CDTQ Report to the General Synod on the Final Report of ARCIC B4.
[23] Southern African Anglican Theological Commission Report on the *Final Report* of ARCIC, II. i. 3.
[24] Standing Committee Appendix B p. 111.
[25] Southern Cone Provincial Theological Commission (English Translation, p. 8).
[26] Response of the Scottish Episcopal Church paras. 8, 9, 10.
[27] Response from the Dioceses of Colombo and Kurunagala.
[28] Cf *Towards a Church of England Response,* p. 77ff
[29] Governing Body of the Church in Wales: the Response of the Doctrinal Commission and of the Provincial Unity Committee to the *Final Report* of ARCIC, p. 23, 24 and 43.
[30] Response from the Church of Melanesia.
[31] Standing Committee Report, p. 126.
[32] Diocesan Responses to the *Final Report* of ARCIC, p. 2.
[33] Church of England Supplementary Report, p. 16.
[34] Response of the Scottish Episcopal Church, p. 7.
[35] *Towards a Church of England Response to BEM and ARCIC,* para. 214, p. 81.
[36] Report of the Standing Commission on Ecumenical Relations on the ARCIC *Final Report,* p. 22.
[37] Responses of the Doctrinal Commission and of the Provincial Unity

Committee to the *Final Report* of ARCIC, p. 45.

[38] Report of the Standing Commission on Ecumenical Relations, p. 23 and 27.

[39] ARCIC *The Final Report* An Australian Response – Summary, p. 3.

[40] Report of the Standing Commission on Ecumenical Relations, p. 25.

[41] Report of the Standing Commission on Ecumenical Relations, p. 26.

[42] CPNZ Commission on Doctrine and Theological Questions, B.3.7.

[43] Report of the Standing Commission on Ecumenical Relations, p. 25.

[44] *Towards a Church of England Response,* p. 89.

[45] Province of the Southern Cone: Provincial Theological Commission Report (English Translation), p. 12.

[46] Southern Cone Theological Commission, p. 13.

[47] Report to the Standing Commission on Ecumenical Relations, p. 7.

[48] Church of Ireland Responses to the *Final Report* of ARCIC I, p. 113.

[49] Cf Church of Ireland Response, p. 145.

[50] An Australian Response, Summary, p. 2.

[51] House of Bishops, NSKK, Jan 1 1987.

[52] Southern Cone Provincial Theological Commission Response, p. 2.

[53] Southern Cone PTCR, p. 2.

[54] Common Declaration 1966, *Final Report,* p. 117

[55] ARCIC-II Agreed Statement, *Salvation and the Church,* CHP/CTS 1987, p. 25.

4
Changes in Anglican-Lutheran Relations

Background and History

The last fifteen years have seen a remarkable convergence between the Lutheran and Anglican Communions. This is true both of theological understanding and of contacts and collaboration. The wider ecumenical movement has provided occasions for more frequent contact between Anglicans and Lutherans. Earlier conversations and resulting varied arrangements for eucharistic sharing between the Church of England and the Scandinavian and Baltic Lutheran Churches contributed. The ecumenical activity and growing self-consciousness of Lutheran and Anglican Churches outside Europe has freed Anglican-Lutheran relations from limited European perspectives, and Lutherans and Anglicans living side by side in some continents share a common mission.

In addition to a growing theological convergence, Lutherans and Anglicans have rediscovered a close affinity. Both emphasise the witness of Holy Scripture as normative and the continuity with the apostolic faith and mission through the centuries, and appreciate the Reformation as a renewal movement within the Catholic Church rather than the beginning of a new Church. Both are marked by high esteem for sacramental life and liturgical worship, and a striking convergence through liturgical revision. Both comprehend convictions and forms of expression which are commonly associated with the 'catholic' and 'protestant' traditions, enabling them to exercise together a mediating role in efforts toward Christian unity. Both have been separated from communion with the Roman Catholic Church, and therefore both regard dialogue with that Church as a major responsibility. Both are in dialogue with the Orthodox, Reformed, and other traditions.

Rapid changes in Anglican-Lutheran relations led the Anglican Consultative Council and the Lutheran World Federation to convene an Anglican-Lutheran Working Group in 1983 to assess the regional dialogues and prepare suitable recommendations. Held in Cold Ash, Berkshire, England, the meeting was marked by a special warmth and a remarkable meeting of minds. The first international dialogue (1970-1972) had produced a report entitled *Anglican-Lutheran International Conversations* (Pullach Report). A Working Group meeting in 1975 to receive comments from the Churches on this report recommended, not a further round of international dialogue, but rather continuation of dialogue and those areas which 'hold special promise and significance in the development of our relations: Europe, United States and Tanzania'.

In the United States the first Lutheran-Episcopal Dialogue (1969-1972) actually began a year before the international dialogue. Its report, *Lutheran-Episcopal Dialogue: A Progress Report* was not acted upon by the Churches. The second dialogue (1976-1980) published *Lutheran-Episcopal Dialogue: Report and Recommendations*. In 1982 after careful preparation the respective General Conventions of three Lutheran Churches (American Lutheran Church, Association of Evangelical Lutheran Churches, Lutheran Church in America) and the Episcopal Church overwhelmingly approved an Agreement in the form of a common resolution. The Agreement established a new relationship between the Episcopal Church and these Lutheran Churches, providing that: (1) on the basis of 'substantial progress' in the reports of the Lutheran-Episcopal Dialogues I and II and of the International Conversations, the Churches look forward, one day, to full communion; (2) they recognise each other as 'Churches in which the Gospel is preached and taught'; (3) they desire to share together in prayer, parochial and diocesan covenants or agreements, Bible study, study of each other's history and tradition, programmes of education and witness, and use of the same buildings; (4) they establish a relationship of 'Interim Sharing of the Eucharist,' and (5) they organise dialogue for discussion of any outstanding questions that must be resolved before full communion, e.g. implications of the gospel, historic episcopate, and ordering of ministries (bishops, priests, and deacons) in the total context of apostolicity.

Interim sharing of the Eucharist is a new term to describe a new relationship on the basis that the teaching of each respective Church is consonant with the Gospel and is sufficiently compatible with the teaching of the others. Interim sharing occurs under two guidelines. First, each Church extends a welcome to the members of the other Churches to receive Holy Communion in it. This welcome 'constitutes a mutual recognition of Eucharistic teaching sufficient for Interim Sharing of the Eucharist, although this does not intend to signify that final recognition of each other's Eucharists or ministries has yet been achieved'. Second, bishops of these Churches may mutually agree to permit 'common, joint celebrations of the Eucharist'. 'The presence of an ordained minister of each participating Church at the altar in this way reflects the presence of two or more Churches expressing unity in faith and baptism as well as the remaining divisions which they seek to overcome; however, this does not imply rejection or final recognition of either Church's Eucharist or ministry.

This is the first bilateral dialogue in which Anglicans participate to have led to formal action in a region based on theological agreement and growth of relationships. The Churches have responded generously with common, joint celebrations of the Eucharist and with slowly increasing numbers of local agreements, study, and action. The third Lutheran-Episcopal Dialogue called for in the Agreement began in 1983.

In Europe discussions between representatives of the Church of England and the Scandinavian Lutheran Churches have continued regularly for over fifty years. Already in 1911 an Anglican report recognised the episcopal succession of the Swedish Church. Since that time various agreements and informal arrangements have led to a sharing in episcopal consecrations in both Churches, to a mutual admission to communion of members in good standing, and to a mutual permission of priests to preach in one another's Churches. Similar arrangements were made with the Latvian and Estonian Lutheran Churches in 1939. All of these Churches have retained an episcopal succession. These arrangements have meant that the Church of England has had a different relationship with these Churches from that it has had with the Churches of Norway, Denmark and Iceland. The Church of England has also had pastoral and theological exchanges with the Evangelical Churches in East and West Germany since the Second World War. This Church brings together Lutheran, Reformed and United Churches.

The Anglican–Lutheran European Commission (1980–1982) published *Anglican-Lutheran Dialogue: The Report of the European Commission* in 1983. It goes beyond the actions resulting from the dialogue in the United States in recommending that full communion be established, but recognises that it will take a time for the report to be received by the Churches, a changed relationship to be implemented by stages, and an agreement on the place of episcopacy to be accepted. Representatives of the Churches in Europe have begun meetings to consider the report, informally so far with the Scandinavian Churches, but formally in 1987 in a consultation with the Evangelical Churches in both East and West Germany.

In Europe, Canada, Latin America, Namibia, Tanzania, Madagascar, Papua New Guinea, and Malaysia there are contacts, co-operation, sharing in social and pastoral work, and mutual participation in worship. In some places such as Australia, Canada, and Tanzania such contacts have led to theological dialogue in order to deepen the contacts, overcome existing issues, and move to degrees of official eucharistic sharing. In other places closer Anglican–Lutheran relations are entirely in the future or initial states. Nevertheless, the overall development is remarkable and constitutes a new and significant stage in the history of the two Communions.

Goals and Steps

The Cold Ash meeting of 1983 also prepared recommendations to the Anglican Consultative Council and the Lutheran World Federation. It described the goal of full communion:

> By full communion we here understand a relationship between two distinct Churches or communions. Each maintains its own autonomy and recognises the catholicity and apostolicity of the other, and each believes the other to hold the essentials of the Christian faith:
>
> (a) 'subject to such safeguards as ecclesial discipline may properly require, members of one body may receive the sacraments of the other;
>
> (b) 'subject to local invitation, bishops of one Church may take part in the consecration of the bishops of the other, thus acknowledging the duty of mutual care and concern;
>
> (c) 'subject to Church regulation, a bishop, pastor/priest or deacon of one ecclesial body may exercise liturgical functions in a congregation of the other body if invited to do so and also, when requested, pastoral care of the other's members;
>
> (d) 'it is also a necessary addition and complement that there should be recognised organs or regular consultation and communication, including episcopal collegiality, to express and strengthen the fellowship and enable common witness, life and services'.

To be in full communion means that Churches become interdependent while remaining autonomous. One is not elevated to be the judge of the other, nor can it remain insensitive to the other; neither is each body committed to every secondary feature of the tradition of the other. Thus the corporate strength of the Churches is enhanced in love, and an isolated independence is restrained.

Full communion carries implications which go beyond sharing the same eucharist. The eucharist is a common meal, and to share in it together has implications for a sharing of life and of common concerns for the mission of the Church. To be in full communion implies a community of life, an exchange and a commitment to one another in respect of major decisions on questions of faith, order, and morals. It implies, where Churches are in the same geographical area, common worship, study, witness, evangelism, and promotion of justice, peace and love. It may lead to a uniting of ecclesial bodies if they are, or come to be, immediately adjacent in the same geographical area. This should not imply the suppressing of ethnic, cultural or ecclesial characteristics or traditions within one communion. (Paragraphs 25-27).

Cold Ash recognised that moving towards full communion will involve steps and stages. One stage is agreement in the faith, to be approved by appropriate juridical authorities of the Churches, reflecting a general consensus within the Churches expressed not only in doctrine but also in common prayer and practical collaboration. Agreed statements can thus provide a basis for mutual recognition of Churches and some degree of interim eucharistic sharing. To reach the goal of full communion, the Churches should reach consensus on authority in the Church, the gospel and its implications, justification/salvation, the sacraments, the ministry and its ordering.

Another stage is to have developed some *modus vivendi* of worship and work. The tentative beginnings of common prayer, study, witness, and evangelism as well as joint projects initiated during the stage of interim eucharistic sharing should have developed greatly and become the norm before the goal of full communion can be reached. Agreement in the faith and recognition of ministries must be accompanied by shared understandings of the gospel and its implications for the life and the words and deeds of the Church.

The recommendations from Cold Ash begin with the affirmation ' . . . in the light of the communion centred around Word and sacrament we have experienced in each other's traditions, we are mutually able to recognise the presence of the Church of Jesus Christ in our respective Communions. This recognition can be affirmed even if there is not as yet complete agreement on the ministerial expressions of apostolicity. But in spite of convergence rather than consensus on this sensitive issue our mutual recognition of Christ prompts us to move with urgency towards the fullest possible ecclesial recognition and the goal of full communion'.

First steps upon the way are recommended: (a) Anglican and Lutheran Churches should officially encourage eucharistic hospitality where pastoral need exists and when ecumenical occasions make this appropriate. (b) The Churches of our two

Communions should make provision for appropriate forms of 'interim eucharistic sharing: along the lines of that authorised in the USA or recommended by the European Regional Commission as a further step towards full communion where there is a commitment to that goal'.

Recommendations to the Anglican Consultative Council and the Lutheran World Federation also include a permanent International Continuation Committee to co-ordinate and assess developing Anglican-Lutheran relationships and dialogues; a joint consultation on Apostolic Succession, the Ministry of the whole People of God, Episcopacy and the Historic Episcopate; and close co-operation on political and social matters of mutual concern. The Cold Ash recommendations were approved by the Anglican Consultative Council and the Lutheran World Federation. The Continuation Committee began work in 1986 and a Consultation on *Episcopé* is planned for 1987.

Response and Reception

We are accustomed to following the progress of dialogues and the production of agreed statements, but we need also to trace the ecclesiastical response. Here is one of the chief difficulties of the dialogues: problems of faith can never be treated simply as problems of faith, for they rapidly become ecclesiastical problems. Anglican-Lutheran dialogue is the first bilateral actually to lead to ecclesiastical decisions concerning teaching and mission. It is the first time that faith, worship, life, and mission are all affected, or potentially affected by ecclesial decisions which are the consequence of bilateral dialogue.

When Lutheran-Episcopal Dialogue II in the USA reported its recommendations, they were studied by the national ecumenical commissions in each of the Churches, and these remained in close touch with each other. In the Episcopal Church selected dioceses also studied the report. Here we note the importance of the pastoral responsibility of elected leaders of dioceses and congregations and consequently of their exercise of that responsibility vis á vis the dialogue report.

But something else took place which turned out to be of paramount importance. The chairman of the national ecumenical commission of the Episcopal Church wrote to the Presiding Bishop informing him of its activity and urging him to consult with the elected heads of the Lutheran Churches. Presiding Bishop, John M. Allin, and Bishop James R. Crumley of the Lutheran Church in America with their ecumenical officers, all in New York City, met periodically to review the situation in the four Churches and plan for the future. Through correspondence and occasional meetings with the heads of the other Lutheran Churches, they were able to give broad pastoral oversight to the entire process from early 1981 until the General Conventions met in four cities in September 1982. The leadership of the heads of the four Churches was unquestionably a major factor leading to the wide approval given by the four conventions and by the people in the Churches afterwards.

While this account of pastoral leadership is drawn from the USA, it should be noted further that the Archbishop of Canterbury was present and spoke to the 1986 Convention of the Lutheran Church in America when it voted to unite with the American Lutheran Church and the Association of Evangelical Lutheran Churches. During the Luther Year, the Archbishop's pastoral leadership extended to visits to Churches in the Federal Republic of Germany and the German Democratic Republic.

Churches in different regions will respond and receive the work of the dialogue in different ways, yet tracing the ecclesiastical response in one region shows how important the Churchly context is. It is clear that the ecclesial context of the dialogues should receive increasing attention. The dialogues themselves need to recognise the necessity of the study of ecclesiology. This is a further illustration of the truth that, under the gospel, mission and unity are integrally related.

Conclusion addressed to Lambeth

Among future tasks in Anglican–Lutheran relations there stand out:

1.   INTERIM EUCHARISTIC SHARING

The Conference should be asked to recognise and command the proposal from the Anglican–Lutheran Working Group to the Provinces that they make appropriate provision for 'interim eucharistic sharing' with Lutheran Churches along the lines of the agreement in the USA, or as recommended by the European Regional Commission, as a step towards full communion.

2.   WHAT DOES IT MEAN TO BE IN FULL COMMUNION?

The Anglican–Lutheran Working Group raised the question of the meaning of the goal of full communion and issued an agreed statement of its understanding. This helps to raise the question for the two Communions as their relationship grows as well as for other communions. The Lambeth Conference should consider responding with a call for a study of communion ecclesiology. Included in the study should be the tension between the Christian demands of being in full communion and the autonomy proper to a Province or Communion.

3.   CONSULTATION ON EPISCOPÉ

Planned for September 1987, the Anglican–Lutheran Consultation on Episcopé is to take up its exercise in the ministry and mission of the Church and specifically in the two Communions. The Conference may consider and comment on the report and commend it for study in the Provinces.

Appendix

Agreement between the American Lutheran Church, the Association of Evangelical Lutheran Churches, the Lutheran

Church in America and the Episcopal Church of the United States of America.

Resolved, that this 67th General Convention of the Episcopal Church:

(1) Welcome and rejoice in the substantial progress of the Lutheran–Episcopal Dialogues (LED) I and II and of the Anglican–Lutheran International Conversations, looking forward to the day when full communion is established between the Anglican and Lutheran Churches;

(2) Recognise now the Lutheran Church in America, the Association of Evangelical Lutheran Churches, and American Lutheran Church as Churches in which the Gospel is preached and taught;

(3) Encourage the development of common Christian life throughout the respective Churches by such means as the following:

(a) Mutual prayer and mutual support, including parochial/ congregational and diocesan/synodical covenants or agreements;

(b) Common study of the Holy Scriptures, the histories and theological traditions of each Church, and the materials of LED I and II;

(c) Joint use of physical facilities;

(4) Affirm now on the basis of studies of LED I and II and of the Anglican–Lutheran International Conversations that the basic teaching of each respective Church is consonant with the Gospel and is sufficiently compatible with the teaching of this Church that a relationship of Interim Sharing of the Eucharist is hereby established between these Churches in the USA under the following guidelines:

(a) The Episcopal Church extends a special welcome to members of these three Lutheran Churches to receive Holy Communion in it under the standard for Occasional Eucharist Sharing of its 1979 General Convention. This welcome constitutes a mutual recognition of eucharistic teaching sufficient for Interim Sharing of the Eucharist, although this does not intend to signify that final recognition of each other's Eucharists or ministries has yet been achieved.

(b) Bishops of Dioceses of the Episcopal Church and Bishops/Presidents of the Lutheran Districts and Synods may by mutual agreement extend the regulations of Church discipline to permit common, joint celebration of the Eucharist within their jurisdictions. This is appropriate in particular situations where the said authorities deem that local conditions are appropriate for the sharing of worship jointly by congregations of the respective Churches. The presence of an ordained minister of each participating Church at the altar in this way reflects the presence of two or more Churches expressing unity in faith and baptism as well as the remaining divisions which they seek to overcome; however, this does not imply rejection or final recognition of either Church's Eucharist or ministry. In such circumstances the eucharistic prayer will be one from the *Lutheran Book of Worship* or the *Book of Common Prayer* as authorised jointly by the Bishop of the Episcopal Diocese and the Bishops/Presidents of the corresponding Lutheran Districts/Synods.

(c) This resolution and experience of Interim Sharing of the Eucharist will be communicated at regular intervals to the other Churches of the Lutheran and Anglican Communions throughout the world, as well as the various ecumenical dialogues in which Anglicans and Lutherans are engaged, in order that consultation may be fostered, similar experiences encouraged elsewhere, and already existing relationships of full communion respected.

(5) Authorise and establish now a third series of Lutheran-Episcopal Dialogues for the discussion of any other outstanding questions that must be resolved before full communion *(communio in sacris/*altar and pulpit fellowship) can be established between the respective Churches, e.g. implications of the Gospel, historic episcopate, and ordering of ministry (Bishops, Priests, and Deacons) in the total context of apostolicity.

5
Anglican/Orthodox Relations

1 Anglican–Orthodox Relations Since 1978

(a) When the Lambeth Conference of 1978 met, Anglican-Orthodox relations were in a critical state. A month before the Anglican-Orthodox Joint Doctrinal Commission had met at Moni Pendeli, Athens and had drawn up a statement on the ordination of women which was distributed to the bishops. It set out the Orthodox position on the subject and the Anglican positions. The Orthodox statement included this paragraph:

> The action of ordaining women to the priesthood involves not simply a canonical point of Church discipline, but the basis of the Christian faith as expressed in the Church's ministries. If the Anglicans continue to ordain women to the priesthood, this will have a decisively negative effect on the issue of the recognition of Anglican orders. Those Orthodox Churches which have partially or provisionally recognised Anglican orders did so on the ground that the Anglican Church has preserved the apostolic succession; and the apostolic succession is not merely continuity in the outward laying on of hands, but signifies continuity in apostolic faith and spiritual life. By ordaining women Anglicans would sever themselves from this continuity, and so any existing acts of recognition by the Orthodox would have to be reconsidered. (*Anglican-Orthodox Dialogue: the Dublin Agreed Statement 1984.* Appendix 2, p. 60.)

The Orthodox members of the Commission hoped the statement would persuade the Conference to discourage the ordination of women in the Churches of the Anglican Communion and so remove a major new obstacle to the reconciliation of Anglicans and Orthodox. The outcome of the Conference in this respect was not satisfactory to the Orthodox, and some participants in the Dialogue thought the Joint Doctrinal Discussions should continue only as 'an academic and informative exercise, and no longer as an ecclesial endeavour aiming at the union of the two Churches' (Archbishop Athenagoras of Thyateira and Great Britain, Orthodox Co-Chairman).

(b) The present Archbishop of Canterbury, then Bishop of St Albans, the Anglican Co-Chairman, visited most of the Orthodox Churches in 1979 and found that most of the Orthodox wished the Dialogue to continue as before. When the Executive Committee of the Discussions met later that year it agreed that the full commission should meet in 1980, in order to resume its work interrupted by the storm over the ordination of women, which had burst upon it in 1977. The Executive Committee affirmed that: 'The ultimate aim remains the unity of the Churches'. It recognised, however, that 'the method may need to change in order to emphasise the pastoral and practical dimensions of the subjects of the theological discussions'. The Committee recognised that unity was a long way off and that 'the discovery of differences on various matters though distressing, will be seen as a necessary step on the long road toward that unity which God wills for his Church'. (Introduction to the *Dublin Agreed Statement.*)

(c) The Commission resumed its work in 1980, and agreed to carry on with its discussion of topics already on the agenda, leaving aside for the time being the question of the ordination of women. In 1984 it produced its second agreed statement at Dublin which now stands alongside the *Moscow Agreed Statement* of 1976. It included sections on: The Mystery of the Church; Faith in the Trinity; Prayer and Holiness; and Worship and Tradition. The Commission did not succeed in taking up the hint in the Executive Committee's report that practical and pastoral dimensions should be given greater prominence. The nearest it came to doing so was in its consideration of the theme of participation in the grace of the Holy Trinity and Christian holiness. This was intended to be a perhaps helpful alternative approach to trinitarian theology and the Filioque, drawing on Christian experience of the grace of the Holy Trinity. It led to the inclusion in the *Dublin Agreed*

Statement of 1984 of the only statement on prayer in any ecumenical text.

(d) In September 1986 an Executive Committee meeting was held to plan the next stage of the Dialogue. The Orthodox expressed a strong desire for the agenda to include those aspects of Christian faith about which there had recently been controversy in the Church of England. The Anglicans were equally clear that the Commission must look more closely at such fundamental questions as freedom and variety within the one tradition of the Church, and the role of scripture and tradition in determining the limits of such freedom and variety. This had been one of the issues facing the Dialogue discerned by the Primates in March 1986. The topics agreed on for the full Commission's meeting in 1987 combine these concerns. Christology and ecclesiology, including the ordination and consecration of women, will be considered as particular instances of the more general issue raised by the Anglicans. It is envisaged that a third Agreed Statement will be drawn up in 1990.

2 The Present State of the Anglican-Orthodox Dialogue

(a) Since the present Joint Doctrinal Discussions began in 1973, it has become clear that the road towards unity between Anglicans and Orthodox will be longer than some perhaps thought at their inception. The conclusion of the Introduction to the *Dublin Agreed Statement* includes this important passage:

> If we accept that Anglican-Orthodox Dialogue is still in the *first* stage of exploring each other's faith and seeking co-operation in mission and service, then it can perhaps be seen that much good work is being done by this particular bilateral conversation to help bridge the ancient divide between the Eastern and Western Churches.

The latter part of this paragraph is as important as the first. Some of the issues which need to be resolved in Anglican-Orthodox Dialogue are issues which arise from the difference between the Christian traditions of East and West. The long-standing friendship between Anglicans and Orthodox, and the absence of any traditional hostility between the two Churches, should enable the Anglican–Orthodox Discussions to make a contribution to the wider process of East-West reconciliation.

(b) The two Agreed Statements so far produced by the Anglican-Orthodox Joint Doctrinal Discussions occupy rather different positions in the two Churches. From the moment they are signed by the Orthodox delegates they have ipso facto an official position in the Orthodox Churches. In the Anglican Communion it rests with each Province to consider the Statements and evaluate them.

(c) The Orthodox Churches reviewed their ecumenical relationships at the Third Panorthodox Preparatory Conference in February 1986. They said this of Anglican-Orthodox Dialogue:

> The third Panorthodox Preparatory Conference considers satisfactory the work so far accomplished by the Joint Doctrinal Commission responsible for the dialogue between the Orthodox and Anglican Churches, and this despite the tendency displayed by the Anglicans to want to minimise this dialogue. The Commission has drawn up agreed texts on Trinitarian theology, ecclesiology, as well as on the life, worship and tradition of the Church.

Orthodox satisfaction with the progress of the dialogue was not unqualified, and the report continues:

> At the same time this Conference notes that the Agreement signed in 1976 at Moscow on the removal of the Filioque from the Creed has not yet had any widespread effect. Similarly, in spite of the discussions and the Declarations made by the Orthodox at Athens (1978) and elsewhere, against the ordination of women, a certain number of Churches of the Anglican Communion, continue to perform such ordinations. These tendencies could have negative consequences for the continuation of the dialogue.

It goes on to express a more general concern:

> A major difficulty for the continuation without reservations of this dialogue stems equally from the flexible and imprecise ecclesiological presuppositions of Anglicans which as such could relativise the

content of agreed theological texts. A similar difficulty arises from the various extremist statements of some Anglican bishops on questions of faith.

(d) The Lambeth Conference of 1978 approved this resolution on Anglican–Orthodox theological dialogue:

1. Welcomes the achievement of the Anglican-Orthodox Joint Doctrinal Commission as expressed in the Moscow Agreed Statement of 1976, and believes that this goes far to realise the hopes about Anglican–Orthodox Dialogue expressed at Lambeth 1968;

2. Requests the Anglican-Orthodox Joint Doctrinal Commission to continue to explore the fundamental questions of doctrinal agreement and disagreement in our Churches; and to promote regional groups for theological dialogue which would bring to the Commission not only reactions to their work, but also theological issues arising out of local experience;

3. Requests that all member Churches of the Anglican Communion should consider omitting the Filioque from the Nicene Creed, and that the Anglican-Orthodox Joint Doctrinal Commission through the Anglican Consultative Council should assist them in presenting the theological issues to their appropriate Synodical bodies and should be responsible for any necessary consultation with other Churches of the Western tradition.

The following year the Anglican Consultative Council re-affirmed its commitment to Anglican–Orthodox dialogue and called for the continuance of the Anglican–Orthodox Joint Doctrinal Discussions at the official and international level. It expressed reservations about the request of the 1978 Lambeth Conference that the Churches of the Anglican Communion consider the omission of the Filioque Clause from the Nicene Creed in accordance with the proposals and understanding of the Moscow Agreed Statement:

The Council has sympathy with this request but is also aware of the danger of this proposal being treated superficially as merely historical or liturgical, rather than theological or spiritual. It also believes, with the Lambeth Conference, that there must be a discussion with other Western Churches and that appropriate material must be prepared to assist the synodical bodies of our Communion to come to a considered judgement. In the meantime the member Churches in their liturgical revisions might well consider ways to indicating that 'This clause is a Western addition to the Creed as originally authorised' (*ACC-4,* p. 4).

It passed the following resolution:

The Council:
1.   Endorses the 1978 Lambeth Conference resolution 35.3 to consider the omission of the Filioque of the Nicene Creed;
2.   Requests the Anglican Members of the Anglican-Orthodox Joint Doctrinal Discussions to prepare explanatory material for use by Synods on both the historical and theological issues involved, noting with interest the Faith and Order Commission of the World Council of Churches' document in preparation, asking the Joint Doctrinal Discussions to take the completed document into consideration, and to be responsible for any necessary consultation with other Churches of the Western tradition;
3.   Recommends that the issue be discussed by the Churches when the explanatory material has been prepared, in the context of a renewal and reaffirmation of the living experience of the one God in Trinity; and a new consideration of the relation of the person and work of the Holy Spirit to the person and work of Christ.

The ACC meeting in 1981 had before it responses to the request of the Lambeth Conference from some of the Provinces, and noted 'that while some are willing to delete the clause and some have already done so, others are cautious even to the point of reluctance. The Episcopal Church in Scotland's reply might be taken as exemplary, that "whatever the Western Churches decide to do, they should do it together".' It passed this resolution (3) on The 'Filioque' Clause in the Nicene Creed:

The Council:
(a)   expresses its gratitude to the members of the Anglican-Orthodox Joint Doctrinal Commission for their work in the past and looks forward to a new report which will enable the two traditions to find practical ways of extending dialogue and co-operation at all levels, especially where the two Churches are living side by side;
(b)   recommends that in discussing the 'Filioque' Clause, the Provinces should, in the exercise of their autonomy, make their decisions with close consideration for the possibility or non-possibility of a final Anglican and Western consensus;

(c)   recommends that within the Provinces there be no unilateral diocesan alteration of the Creed;

(d)   recommends that latitude might be allowed for deviations from this policy on rare and exceptional occasions of ecumenical courtesy towards the Orthodox Churches; and

(e)   requests the Secretary General to keep the matter under review in preparation for the next Lambeth Conference.

The 1984 meeting of the Council, which took place not long before the Dublin meeting of the Anglican-Orthodox Joint Doctrinal Commission, commended 'the forthcoming Agreed Statement in the hope that it will be widely studied, not least in parishes where the two traditions are found together, and become a stimulus for local Anglican-Orthodox collaboration'.

3 Lambeth 1988 and the Anglican-Orthodox Dialogue

(a)   It is important for the continuation of the dialogue that the Lambeth Conference should re-affirm the commitment of the Anglican Communion to the Joint Doctrinal Discussions with the Orthodox Church. There is a feeling among the Orthodox that Anglicans wish to minimise the importance of the dialogue, and that preference is being given over this, the first of the international dialogues to which Orthodox and Anglicans committed themselves, to more recent and perhaps apparently more fruitful dialogues. The Conference will certainly want to re-affirm its commitment to an ecumenical endeavour embracing all Churches willing to participate in it. But it would be of great assistance to Anglican-Orthodox relations if it could at the same time make clear that it attaches no less importance to this particular dialogue than formerly. In 1988 the Russian Orthodox Church will celebrate the millennium of the conversion of the Kievan Russian state to Christianity, a fact of which the Conference may wish to take note and which it could use as an opportunity for expressing Anglican appreciation of the friendly relations which have

always existed between the Russian and other Orthodox Churches and Anglicans.

(b) Anglican-Orthodox dialogue is important for several reasons. It was the first East-West dialogue to be established, and is making a contribution not only to Anglican-Orthodox but to East-West Christian growth towards understanding and reconciliation. At the same time it is one more means of contact between peoples of East and West, and so has a part to play in forging links between peoples politically divided. Precisely because it is a dialogue between an Eastern and a Western Christian tradition it has to face and try to overcome difficulties that do not exist in dialogues between Western Churches. Yet if it is true that each of the two traditions has its own indispensable contribution to make to the fullness of the Church, those difficulties must not be allowed to obscure the essential nature of this particular ecumenical task. Moreover, it is no longer the case that the Anglican and Orthodox Churches are remote from one another geographically. In many parts of the world there is an Orthodox diaspora making Orthodox communities close neighbours with Anglicans. In some places converts to Orthodoxy make up a significant proportion of local Orthodox congregations. While this fact, and differences of cultural background, make local relationships difficult to build up, the fact that Orthodoxy is now a permanent part of the Christian community in areas of predominantly Western Christian tradition makes it impossible for a genuine ecumenical concern to ignore or minimise its significance. For centuries, too, Orthodox Christians have lived in, or on the border with, Islamic societies, and in the present century have had to learn to live and witness in militant atheistic societies. They need the encouragement of Western Christians more fortunately placed, while the latter can learn much from their experience.

(c) In affirming its commitment to the dialogue, the Conference needs to consider how the Anglican Communion is to respond to the work so far accomplished by the Joint Doctrinal Commission, and in particular to its proposal concerning the

Filioque. The *Moscow Agreed Statement* seems never to have been commended to the Provinces, although ACC-6 did commend in advance the *Dublin Agreed Statement* for study. Neither of the two statements makes any specific recommendation, except as regards the Filioque. Nor are they entirely statements of doctrine with which all members of the Commission agree, and which they submit to their respective Churches for their consideration. They include such statements, which form the greater part of both texts. But they also include sections setting out the divergent beliefs of Orthodox and Anglicans. The Epilogue to the *Dublin Agreed Statement* lists those points on which agreement has been reached and those which require further exploration. The Statements cannot therefore be treated in quite the same way as the *Final Report* of ARCIC I.

Yet some response is needed if the momentum of the dialogue is to be maintained. It would be helpful if a process could be initiated whereby Provinces could state their views on those sections of the Statements which were agreed by both Anglican and Orthodox members of the Commission. This would at least ensure that the Statements were given serious attention by all the Provinces, and would clarify which areas of agreement reached by the Commission had the endorsement of the Provinces. It has been suggested that the Provinces might be asked to say whether or not such parts of the Statements were 'sufficiently consonant in substance with the faith of this Church to justify further conversations with a view to the eventual reconciliation of our Churches grounded in agreement in faith'. It has to be recognised that the kind of intermediate steps envisaged in the growth towards unity of Anglicans and some other Churches are not at present conceivable in relations with the Orthodox.

(d) The one definite proposal which has emerged from the Anglican-Orthodox dialogue concerns the restoration of the Nicene Creed to its original form. The recommendation of the Anglican members of the Commission made in the *Moscow Agreed Statement* of 1976 that Filioque should not be included in

this creed was reaffirmed in the *Dublin Agreed Statement*. The responses on the part of the Provinces to the 1978 Lambeth Conference's resolution on the subject are summarised below. The disappointment of the Orthodox that no action has been taken by the Anglican Communion as a whole was expressed in the Panorthodox Preparatory Conference's Statement on Anglican-Orthodox Relations. The Episcopal Church of the USA has requested that the 1988 Lambeth Conference should collate the results of Provincial discussions and if possible make a pronouncement on the subject. There is no doubt that if the Provinces of the Communion were to restore the Nicene Creed to its original form a major difficulty in Anglican-Orthodox relations would have been removed.

(e) The Orthodox have indicated that they consider ecclesiology should occupy a prominent place in the next stage of the dialogue. The *Dublin Agreed Statement* may fairly be held to have made an important contribution to this theme in its section on the mystery of the Church. Important areas of it remain to be discussed further, not least the question of primacy. A key issue is that of the limits of the Church. The *Dublin Agreed Statement* notes that 'Anglicans are accustomed to seeing our divisions as within the Church: they do not believe that they alone are the one true Church, but they believe that they belong to it. Orthodox, however, believe that the Orthodox Church is the one true Church of Christ, which as his Body is not and cannot be divided. But at the same time they see Anglicans as brothers and sisters in Christ who are seeking with them the union of all Christians in the one church' (*Dublin Agreed Statement* p. 11). The Lambeth Conference may wish to underline this as a basic issue which needs to be resolved before any significant progress towards the reconciliation of the two Churches.

(f) However much encouragement the Lambeth Conference may give to Anglican-Orthodox dialogue, its next stage is unlikely to be easy. The consecration of women to the episcopate, should it take place, will certainly create a furore not less than that evoked among the Orthodox by their

ordination to the priesthood. The doctrinal views of some Anglicans will continue to upset the Orthodox. It will be necessary to recall that Anglicans and Orthodox are still in the first stages of exploring each other's faith. Anglicans need to keep in mind the fact that some at least of the bewilderment and apparent anger of the Orthodox at developments within Anglicanism which place further obstacles in the way of good relations stems from their earlier assumption that the Anglican Church was the closest to them of all the non-Orthodox Western Churches. They react the more vigorously to the discovery of hitherto unsuspected differences and to the emergence of fresh obstacles. Nor will the dialogue be helped by the growing anti-ecumenical sentiment in some Orthodox circles. This is largely an anti-Western movement and affects Roman Catholic-Orthodox dialogue perhaps even more than Anglican-Orthodox. These difficulties at the level of official dialogue need to be offset by encouraging personal contacts and friendships, and regional and local dialogues and contacts between local parish communities, where Anglicans and Orthodox live alongside each other.

Appendix

RESPONSES TO THE RESOLUTION OF ACC-4 ON THE FILIOQUE CLAUSE

The Church in *Burma* has removed the Filioque from the Creed.

Canada The General Synod in June 1980 'notes with approval that the new Third Canadian Eucharist omits the Filioque Clause in the Nicene Creed, thus restoring the original text: we understand this action to be in response to the Lambeth Conference Resolution 35 part 3, and made at the request of the Eastern Orthodox Churches. We express the hope that all future revisions of Canadian Liturgies follow this example, while leaving present formularies intact. This action implies no change in the doctrine expressed in Article 5 of the Thirty-Nine Articles contained in the Book of Common Prayer'.

England The Archbishop of Canterbury's Filioque Commission reported in 1976. But the General Synod's Liturgical Revision Committee rejected a proposal to place the words 'and Son' in brackets in the 1980 Alternative Service Book, as it was felt to be a doctrinal rather than a liturgical matter. The House of Bishops was also unwilling to deal with the matter 'by amendments in a liturgical debate' and declined therefore to recommend its deletion, or its being put in parenthesis, or even a note to explain 'that this clause is a Western addition to the Creed as originally authorised', for fear that if a proposal at *that* stage was rejected by the Synod, the only course open would be to reject the whole Alternative Service Book. However in May 1981 the House of Bishops discussed the matter and the Archbishop of Canterbury made a speech on the subject to the July Synod on a 'take note' motion. Since then the Church of England has supported the setting up by the British Council of Churches of the Study Commission on Trinitarian Doctrine Today whose brief includes the Filioque and which is due to report in 1988.

Australia referred the matter to its Doctrine Commission, which made a statement in 1981 which emphasised that the real issue at stake is that of authority: 'who has the right to add to, and delete from, the only truly ecumenical Creed?' It points out the appropriateness of the Filioque in relation to the *mission* of the Holy Spirit, as is shown by Epiphanius, Ephraem and Cyril of Alexandria as well as Tertullian, Hilary, and Augustine; and recommends (a) that the Churches of the Anglican Communion act in concert on this matter and (b) that the Australian Church's Canon Law Commission be asked to investigate the constitutional implications of any move to delete the Filioque from the Nicene Creed.

The Church of the Province of Southern Africa at Provincial Synod, November, 1982 resolved:

> This Synod noting developments within the Anglican and Roman Catholic Communions since 1979, agrees to the principle that the Nicene Creed should be recited omitting the Filioque Clause for the following reasons:
> 1. that in this form, it is a right statement of the Christian faith concerning the eternal relationships within the Godhead;
> 2. that we see this as a gesture of love and reconciliation towards our brothers in the Eastern Church;
> 3. that it is a concession to the inadequacy of language and the difficulty of accurate translation into the various South African languages.

The Episcopal Church of the United States of America at General Convention in 1985 voted for its removal provided the Lambeth Conference requested this of the Communion in 1988.

Nippon Sei Ko Kai The House of Bishops in February 1979 welcomed the possibility of further discussion, consultation, and investigation on the Filioque.

The Church of the Province of Tanzania The House of Bishops accepted the following recommendation of the Provincial Theological and Doctrinal Board in 1982:

> that the Province would not accept the omission of the clause, as to do so raised important doubts on the Doctrine of the Trinity. There is also theological and scriptural evidence to confirm that the Holy Spirit comes from the Father and the Son (John 14.26, 15.26, 16.7,13 Matthew 3.16, 2 Corinthians 13.14).

However the Bishops held themselves open to further consideration of the subject.

The Church in Wales Doctrine Commission was ready to reconsider the matter after receiving the report of the Faith and Order Commission of the World Council of Churches.

The Church of the Province of the West Indies resolved:
that this Synod of the Province of the West Indies now in session in
Antigua in 1979 hereby agrees to omit the Filioque Clause from the
Nicene Creed in both modern and traditional forms in present and
future printings of the experimental liturgy of this Province.

OTHER WESTERN CHURCHES

The Roman Catholic Church With a letter of 16 February
1981, Father Pierre Duprey of the Secretariat for Promoting
Christian Unity has sent a short paper on the Filioque which
accepts that it is an addition to the original text of the Creed,
but without questioning or denying the truth of the doctrine it
expresses, notes that there is no Filioque in the Greek texts of
the Latin rite Church in Greece, principally because 'procedere'
is a more general, and 'ekporeuein' a more specific word;
emphases the pastoral problem of explaining that omission on
canonical grounds does *not* involve any change in doctrine;
notes the need for full consultation between the several
Western Churches, rather than one taking such a step on its
own; and speaks of 'a pluralism of expression — even in the
Creed' but without 'fundamental divergence of faith'.

The Church of Scotland's 'Panel on Doctrine' in May 1979
examined the question very fully and its report recommended
to the General Assembly above all that 'whatever the Western
Churches decide to do, they should do it together'.

The World Alliance of Reformed Churches The Chairman
and Secretary of its Department of Theology wrote in
November 1980 to explain that the World Alliance of
Reformed Churches 'has not as yet formally taken up this
issue, but . . . it would be probable that the majority of our 147
member Churches on the six continents would adopt the
position outlined in the Faith and Order Paper'. However 'we
question if unilateral action by one communion alone would be
the most helpful way forward. . . Could we not envisage the
use of existing ecumenical structures, e.g. the Faith and Order

Commission . . . in such a way that the separate decision making authoritative structures of the different Churches be invited to make their decisions known in a corporate manner together?'

The Lutheran World Federation Dr Günther Gassmann, at that time on the staff of the Lutheran World Federation, expressed the opinion in 1982 that Western Churches should move together on this question.

World Council of Churches The Faith and Order Commission's current work on an 'Ecumenical Explication of the Apostolic Faith as Expressed in the Nicene-Constantinopolitan (381) Creed' is based on the original text.

6
Anglican–Oriental Orthodox Relations

Describing the context of the life and witness of the Oriental Churches, the Archbishop of Canterbury, Dr Robert Runcie recently said:

> Your Churches are at the interface of some of the greatest issues facing the world today. Christianity and Islam face each other as there is an increasing stridency in the followers of the Prophet which makes dialogue more difficult than in former years.
>
> In India there is a wider encounter with other faiths, as well as the new phenomenon of a third world secularism.
>
> In Ethiopia the Church seeks to play its part in the alleviation of one of the greatest famines of modern times. In that country and also in Armenia, the Church must find a way of working alongside a theoretically Marxist and atheist state.
>
> In the Lebanon we see the tragedy of the disintegration of a state in the pressures of competing ideologies and neighbouring powers. Anglicans salute your witness.[1]

He was speaking at the conclusion of the Anglican–Oriental Orthodox Forum in Canterbury, October 1985.

The Forum was the beginning of a more systematic exchange between the Anglican Communion and the family of Oriental Orthodox Churches — the Syrian, Coptic, Armenian, Ethiopian, and Malankara (India) Orthodox Churches. Because of the dispersed nature of authority and inter-Church co-operation within the Oriental Orthodox family (a situation not entirely unfamiliar to Anglicans), meetings of the entire family of representatives have been infrequent. The Forum therefore marked the beginning of an important process of systematic exchange between the Anglican Communion and Oriental Orthodox Churches.

No exchange arises out of, and takes place in, a vacuum. Some account, therefore, of the background to the modern position needs to be given.

The Historical Content

Anglicans have a history of good relations with the Oriental Orthodox Churches. These relations go back, in the main, to the beginning of the nineteenth century, but Anglicans were brought into contact with the Syrian Orthodox Church in India as early as the end of the seventeenth century. From 1810-1836 in South India, an important joint venture took place between the CMS and the Syrian Orthodox Church. Described as a 'mission of help', the venture took the form of a jointly run theological college. This form of educational assistance, always on the understanding of the following of a strict 'non-proselytising' policy, has been characteristic of Anglican-Oriental Orthodox exchange. Mutual support, scholarly research, and a refusal to proselytise have thus characterised the exchange at its best. Notions of cultural and racial superiority, and collusion with the forces of Imperial Power have occasionally characterised the exchange at its worst. A major difficulty in the progress of relations between Anglicans and Oriental Orthodox has been lack of continuity. Relations have characteristically depended on the enthusiasm of amateurs with the time (and often, finance) to pursue such matters. Political expediency has often been a factor in the state of relations from the Oriental perspective. In a survey of Anglican-Oriental Orthodox relations, therefore, much is sporadic, but the Lambeth Conferences provide a pointer to the condition of understanding between the two families. Not all the Lambeth Conferences provide detailed information, and consequently only the most important are referred to.

Lambeth 1888 — The third Lambeth Conference

Relations with the Oriental Orthodox Churches were thought to have been of sufficient importance to the Conference to merit a specific item on the Agenda. 'In regard to Eastern communities such as the Coptic, Abyssinian, Syrian, and Chaldean, your committee was clear that our position in the East involves some obligation.'[2] Anglican contact with Oriental Orthodox Churches was invariably in the wake of the spread of British Imperial power. Nevertheless, deeper reasons motivated the exchange than mere physical proximity.

Bishop Brooke Foss Westcott wrote in 1892 of the Anglican interest in the Oriental Churches — 'The interest is natural. These independent Churches appeal with especial force to England and the Churches of the Anglican Communion. . . It (the Anglican Church) is in no temptation to seek either submission or uniformity from those whom it serves. It acknowledges the power of the Faith to harmonise large differences of liturgical and ritual expression, answering to differences of race and history, within the limits of the historic Creed.'[3]

Lambeth 1908 Resolutions 63-65 of the Conference recommended a closer co-operation with the Oriental Orthodox. The Conference recommended that the term 'monophysite' should not be used of the Churches, and went on, 'these struggling Christian Churches, each and all of which have often turned towards us for help, have a real claim upon our love and sympathy.'[4] The Conference also recommended theological talks with the aim of intercommunion, dependent on a 'carefully and sympathetically framed statement of Faith as to Our Lord's Person.'

In 1908, the Syrian Patriarch Abdallah and Bishop John Wordsworth of Salisbury issued such a joint statement of faith.[5]

Lambeth 1920 This was the Conference which produced most concrete material on relations between the Oriental Orthodox Churches and the Anglican Communion. This points to the need for sustained consistency in furthering relations. Randall Davidson had been Archbishop of Canterbury since 1903, and had pursued Oriental Orthodox matters with interest and vigour. Resolutions 22 and 23 reaffirm those of 1908, and press forward with the statement of the need for 'occasional intercommunion.'

Lambeth 1930 This Conference went further in its claim that it 'earnestly desired that these relations may be steadily strengthened, in consultation with the Orthodox Church, in the hope that in due course full intercommunion may be reached.'

Since 1930, the Lambeth Conferences of 1948 and 1958 have concentrated less on the Oriental Orthodox. This, to some measure, reflects the withdrawal of British power from those regions where Oriental Orthodox Churches are strong — principally India and the Middle East. The period has been marked by the strong renewal of monastic and liturgical life in many of the Oriental Orthodox Churches, and by the emergence of an Oriental Orthodox diaspora in the West.

Recent Developments in Dialogue

No exchanges take place in a vacuum and recent conversations have thus a history of co-operation and understanding. The more recent conversations have concentrated on pastoral co-operation, and the developments can be catalogued chronologically.

1.   The WCC Assembly in Vancouver 1983 was the occasion for the Anglican representatives to meet with Oriental Orthodox representatives.

2.   Bishop Henry Hill's (Canada) visits to the Heads of the Oriental Orthodox Churches on behalf of the Anglican Communion were noted with appreciation. The visits continued until the Anglican-Oriental Orthodox Forum.

3.   The Anglican-Oriental Orthodox Forum met in St Albans in October 1985. The Coptic, Syrian, Armenian, Ethiopian and Malankara Orthodox Churches were represented, with an observer from the Assyrian Church of the East. The Forum's agenda was largely pastoral co-operation, and

resulted in three recommendations for further action and developments:

(a)   Theological Scholarships — it was requested that appropriate mechanisms be set up for systematic exchange between Churches of the Anglican Communion and Oriental Orthodox Churches. The haphazard nature of exchanges in the past was noted.

(b)   Regional Pastoral Support — in situations where one Church found itself in the majority, with the other Church(es) as small diasporas, appropriate pastoral support should be given. Specific examples were cited. Education at a general level was noted as important in this area. Television, radio, and publishing should be used to publicise the situation and history of the communities of Oriental Orthodox. *Light from the East* a book of essays on the Oriental Churches is due to be published later this year (1987).

(c)   Theological Conversations — preparations should be made for a future forum focusing on ecclesiological and theological concerns.

4.   The recommendations were sent to all Heads of Churches and the responses recorded by a small Monitoring Group based in London. Positive responses are recorded to date (March 1987) from all Heads of Churches with the exception of Ethiopia which has not yet responded. All encouraged the setting up of a subsequent forum to include discussion on theological conversations.

The Contemporary Context

In the cities of the West, the world is now present. Multi-racial, multi-religious conurbations such as Chicago, Los Angeles, New York, London, Toronto, Birmingham are the setting for the majority of people. Rapid emigration from the Middle East now means that all the Oriental Orthodox communities are represented in countries and cities which had previously been homogeneous. Ignorance of these Churches' language, liturgy and tradition needs to be countered by sound yet accessible literature. Pastoral co-operation can be given to communities struggling to establish themselves. It is likely that the political situation will continue to deteriorate in the Middle East in the foreseeable future. Ecumenical sharing on the ecclesiastical level is thus firmly in the context of the human search for unity.

Recommendations to ACC-7 and the Lambeth Conference 1988

(1)   The general context of the Anglican-Oriental Orthodox exchange should be noted.

(2)   Affirmation of those Churches undergoing severe difficulties in particular in the Middle East needs to be articulated. The Armenian Catholicos of Cilicia wrote in March 1986:

It is a commonly known fact that today we are facing a very decisive time in the history of the Middle East in general and of the Christian Churches therein in particular. You are well aware of the many and complex problems that we are confronting today vis à vis the resurgence of Moslem integrism, the growing pace of Western secular influence, the activities of new Christian fundamentalist groups coming from the West, the movement of emigration of Christians from this area, the social needs of the people resulting from the war situation, and the need for renewal of the local, indigenous Churches of this area, the mission of the Churches *today* and other aspects of the present-day situation. All these and related issues should be seen in situations which are quite different from those that our fathers or the generations before us faced.

The Anglican Communion is one of the Churches that has had a special link with the Middle East. I know well that the Church of England and other member Churches of the Anglican Family continue to witness in this area. It is my firm conviction that discussions, closer consultation with the Oriental Orthodox Churches are called for specifically on these matters of common ecumenical concern.

(3)   The Anglican-Orthodox Forum recommendations to be noted and commended to the Provinces for implementation.

(4)   A future Forum (to be held in 1989/1990), which would include theological talks, to be recommended by ACC 7. Note needs to be taken of theological talks already embarked upon. Chalcedonian Orthodox and non-Chalcedonian Orthodox conversations are recorded in *Does Chalcedon Divide or Unite?* (WCC 1981) and Roman Catholic-Oriental Orthodox discussions recorded in the *Joint Declaration of Pope John Paul II and Syrian Orthodox Patriarch of Antioch* (June 1984) and in the agreement between *Pope Shenouda III (Alexandria) and Pope John Paul II.*

NOTES
[1]   Speech of Welcome of Dr Robert Runcie, Canterbury Cathedral, October 1985
[2]   Report of the Lambeth Conference of 1888
[3]   B. F. Westcott in O. H. Parry, *Six Months in a Syrian Monastery* (1892) p. viii
[4]   Report of the Lambeth Conference of 1908
[5]   Published as *Interview at the Palace (1908)*

7
Anglican-Reformed Relations: God's Reign and Our Unity

(Numbers by quotations from *God's Reign and Our Unity* refer to the paragraph numbering in the Report.)

Formal responses to this Dialogue are only just beginning to come in. This for two reasons: (a) The heavy programme imposed on Churches by ARCIC and BEM (b) The Report itself does not clearly call for an international response and since it is addressed to Reformed, Presbyterian and Congregational ecclesiologies, as well as to the variety of Anglicanism, it becomes clear that local relations will vary from place to place. The Report sets out to facilitate such relations.

God's Reign and Our Unity is therefore unlike ARCIC for which relations at the universal, or Communion level are to a degree determinative of Provincial relations. The Report begins by noting the successful unions in the Indian sub-continent, but the failure of subsequent attempts to unite elsewhere. It states that the Dialogue was called to investigate common ground which could be claimed by Anglican and Reformed Churches seeking greater unity. 'But since that ultimate aim (the great catholic unity of the Body of Christ) cannot be achieved in one great leap, it is proper to ask that Churches should at all times be prepared to look for opportunities for small advances towards it.' (*God's Reign and Our Unity* (2)). The Introduction concludes by noting that the Dialogue took place in the context of daily worship. 'It is only as we meet in adoration of our one Lord, that our minds are drawn into unison' (5).

After noting the different self-understanding of the two families as a factor in keeping us apart, it emphasises that the major impediment is a static concept of the Church. 'Our Report is written in the conviction that the Church is to be understood in a much more dynamic way, as a pilgrim people called to a journey whose goal is nothing less than God's blessed Kingdom, embracing all nations and all creation, a sign, instrument and foretaste of God's purpose 'to sum up all things with Christ as head' (Ephesians 1.10)(14). In denoting the Church as 'sign, instrument and foretaste of the Kingdom', the Report avails itself of the growing understanding of the nature of the Church in ecumenical circles over the past thirty years. It is interesting to note the adoption of this phrase by other Anglican dialogues e.g. Anglican-Orthodox.

If the Kingdom embraces both human and cosmic unity, this unity can only be brought about by the peace and justice of God, which is centred on the Cross. Such a statement is empty unless it is 'embodied (even if only provisionally) in a visible community in which the righteousness of God and the peace of God are actually known and experienced in reality, even though it is only a foretaste of the full reality' (18). Only a reconciled community can be a reconciling community.

Fundamental to the whole Report is God's love poured out through Christ's redeeming work which makes us all 'debtors to grace'. All that we do in obedience to Christ is enabled by and a response to that work. That work was for all mankind, so that our work is apostolic, sent by God to the world to bring about the Kingdom.

The Report goes on to consider life in the Church as requiring both orthodoxy and orthopraxy. Orthodoxy is both true teaching and true worship, rooted in the mystery of the Trinity, but orthodoxy must issue in right action (ortho-praxy). The life of the Church addresses the reality of the world.

Drawing from BEM, the Report sees Baptism, and Eucharist as constitutive of the Church. Both ARCIC and Reformed-Roman Catholic Reports are quoted and this section establishes a broad common ecumenical ground and ecclesiology.

Up to this point the Report draws together much ecumenical work of the previous fifty years and already quotations from the Report in ecumenical writing show that the Commission's work is widely appreciated. It now goes on to consider the more contested ground of patterns and forms of ministry. Here it begins with Christ's call to others to follow him and in particular the appointment of twelve 'to be with him and that he might send them out to preach and have authority to cast out demons' (Mark 3.13ff) (73). 'The company gathered behind closed doors on that first Easter evening was the Church in embryo. It is to the whole Church that the commission is given and it is to the whole Church that the gift of the Spirit is made. The Church as a whole is constituted by this act of sending and anointing' (74). But the same company was also the ministry in embryo. From the beginning there is a pattern of ministerial leadership, neither prior to the Church, nor developed from the Church. 'Leadership of the Church means leading others into the company of Jesus so that – in him and by the working of the Spirit – their lives may be offered to the Father, and also leading others into the world to challenge the dominion of evil in the name of Christ and in the power of the Spirit' (76).

'Order is love in regulative operation' (82) and in ordaining the Church provides for continuity and entrusts authority to the ordained person to act focally and representatively for the whole Church (86).

Noting that neither episcopacy, nor presbyterian order can be read directly out of Scripture, it suggests that episcopacy has the sanction of long tradition, and remains the order of the greater number of Christians to this day. From *Baptism, Eucharist and Ministry,* it insists that ministry must be personal, collegial and communal – a person supported by a college of assistants, and helped in governance by the community.

In considering the differences between Anglican and Reformed Church Order, the Report is more tentative largely because these have to be worked out between particular Churches in particular places. It is here that the Report has run into most criticism, but most of those criticisms result from a failure to take into account the carefully balanced ecclesiology set out in the body of the Report.

Perhaps the most important section of the Report is the final chapter on Our Goal. Noting that earlier divisions were in the main geographical, for the past few centuries we have come to accept different denominations living alongside each other. The idea of such denominations continuing their existence, even though reconciled, is firmly rejected, and the Report adopts the Nairobi vision of a 'conciliar fellowship of local Churches which are themselves truly united'. It admits that modern society raises difficult questions about what is local in large, pluriform cities, with their complexes of interrelated communities. It quotes the WCC Report *In Each Place*. 'The area to be served may vary in size. It may be a village or a small town; it may be a city or part of a city. It should not be so large that the Christian community loses coherence, nor yet so small that its homogeneity favours separatism in the human community. The area should be so chosen that the power of the Gospel to cross human barriers will be made manifest.' The Report ends by hoping that it will be taken up by local groups of Churches and studied in conjunction with BEM and warns that motivation for unity has to spring out of concern for the Kingdom and a readiness to change in obedience to God's call.

8
The Responses of the Anglican Communion to Baptism, Eucharist and Ministry (the Lima Text)

1.   The dialogues we have considered so far have been between two partners. *Baptism, Eucharist and Ministry (the Lima Text)*, the work of the Faith and Order Commission of the World Council of Churches, comes from the most representative ecumenical forum. The earlier fear of bilaterals becoming an independent ecumenical method in competition with the multilateral dialogue has receded with the publication of the texts. There is a growing appreciation that both bilateral and multilateral work serve the one ecumenical movement. The simultaneous publication of many of the texts has shown the close interrelation between bilaterals and the multilateral dialogue. The *Lima Text* has itself profited from the method and insights of the bilaterals and an increasing number of bilaterals refer explicitly to the work of the multilateral. The Anglican-Reformed and the Anglican-Lutheran dialogues, for example, refrain from duplicating work in the areas of baptism and eucharist and affirm the stated consensus of parts of the *Lima Text*. Moreover, the *Lima Text* provides an important over-arching framework in which to position the results of any one bilateral dialogue. What is agreed between two Churches in the area of sacraments and ministry can be set within the emerging convergence arrived at together by many Christian traditions. There are, however, differences between the two forms of dialogue. Some, though not all of the bilaterals, are consciously aiming at 'concrete steps' in the near future. The multilateral is concerned rather with a mutual rediscovery

which has implications both for the renewal of one's own traditions as well as for improving relations in general. However, bilateral and multilateral are both concerned with the search for sufficient agreement in faith to draw the Churches into visible unity.

The Goal of Unity in the Work of the World Council of Churches

2.   The *Lima Text* is one contribution in the search for sufficient theological agreement in faith to sustain the visible unity of the Church. Assembly statements from New Delhi (1961) onwards have been concerned to call the Churches to the goal of visible unity and the Assembly statements have been gradually putting content into the phrase 'visible unity':

(a)   The Third Assembly in New Delhi said this about the form of visible unity;

> We believe that the unity which is both God's will and his gift to his Church is made visible as all in each place who are baptised into Jesus Christ and confess him as Lord and Saviour are brought by the Holy Spirit into one fully committed fellowship, holding the one apostolic faith, preaching the one Gospel, breaking the one bread, joining the common prayer, and having a corporate life reaching out in witness and service to all and who at the same time are united with the whole Christian fellowship in all places and all ages in such wise that ministry and members are accepted by all, and that all can act and speak together as occasion requires for the tasks to which God calls his people.

3.   *(b)   The Fourth Assembly at Uppsala* (1968) developed further certain aspects of this earlier description. It attempted to define more precisely the unity we seek through the use of the concept of conciliarity and to show how the Churches in all places belong together and are called to act together. The Assembly said:

> The Ecumenical movement helps to enlarge this experience of universality, and its regional councils and its World Council may be regarded as a transitional opportunity for eventually actualizing a truly universal, ecumenical conciliar form of common life and

witness. The members of the World Council of Churches, committed to each other, should work for the time when a genuinely ecumenical council may once more speak for all Christians and lead the way into the future (Uppsala Report, p. 17).

4. Uppsala's contribution to the goal of visible unity lay both in its emphasis upon 'conciliar fellowship' and in its emphasis upon the Church as 'sign'. 'The Church is bold in speaking of itself as the sign of the coming unity of humankind.' The emphasis in Uppsala on 'sign' implied that unity does not consist in outward structures, but is a quality to be displayed by the Church in each given situation. That quality has its model, more than that, its source in the life of the Triune God and in the self-giving love of the incarnate Christ.

5. *(c)* In the years between Uppsala and the *Fifth Assembly in Nairobi* (1975) Uppsala's concept of 'conciliar fellowship' was developed in the work of the Faith and Order Commission so that the Nairobi Assembly was able to clarify the concept further:

> The one Church is to be envisioned as a conciliar fellowship of local Churches which are themselves truly united. In this conciliar fellowship each local Church possesses, in communion with the others, the fullness of catholicity, witnesses to the same apostolic faith and therefore recognizes the others as belonging to the same Church of Christ and guided by the same Spirit. They are bound together because they have the same baptism, and share in the same eucharist; they recognize each other's members and ministries. They are one in their common commitment to confess the Gospel of Christ by proclamation and service to the world. To this end each Church aims at maintaining sustained and sustaining relationships with her sister Churches, expressed in conciliar gatherings whenever required for the fulfilment of their common calling (Nairobi Report, p. 60).

6. Nairobi was not setting up an alternative to the model of New Delhi, but drawing out one of its implications. Christians will know that they are truly united in the same Church and are guided by the same Spirit when they realize at least *three* basic

marks of 'conciliar fellowship': consensus in the apostolic faith; mutual recognition of baptism, eucharist, ministry and members; conciliar gatherings for common deliberations and decision.

7.   *(d) The Vancouver Assembly* (1982) recommitted itself to the goal of visible unity. The Report of section 2 again underlined the three characteristics of a united Church:

First, the Churches would share a common understanding of the apostolic faith, and be able to confess this message together in ways understandable, reconciling and liberating to their contemporaries. Living this apostolic faith together, the Churches help the world to realize God's design for creation.

Second, confessing the apostolic faith together, the Churches would share a full mutual recognition of baptism, the eucharist and ministry, and be able through their visible communion to let the healing and uniting power of these gifts become more evident amidst the divisions of humankind.

Third, the Churches would agree on common ways of decision-making and ways of teaching authoritatively, and be able to demonstrate qualities of communion, participation and corporate responsibility which could shed healing light in a world of conflict (Vancouver Report, p. 45).

8.   Over and above this the Report emphasizes the relation of the unity of the Church and the renewal of human community, picking up the Uppsala stress on the Church as 'sign'. 'The Church is called to be a "prophetic sign", a prophetic community through which and by which the transformation of the world can take place.'

9.   The goal of visible unity of the Church can be thus traced in the statements of successive Assemblies of the World Council. The work of the Faith and Order Commission is concerned to develop and deepen the understanding of the three characteristics of a visibly united Church. The *Lima Text* with its work on baptism, eucharist and ministry is the most developed part of this three part agenda. Currently the Commission is engaged in developing work on the *Common*

Expression of the Apostolic Faith Today and is giving some attention to *common structures of decision making and teaching authoritatively*. Work on all three parts of the agenda is influenced by the study of the unity of the Church and the renewal of human community.

10. The publication of the *Lima Text* on Baptism, Eucharist and Ministry in January 1982 marked the end of a process of theological dialogue which began at the First World Faith and Order Conference in Lausanne in 1927. The number of Churches represented in the work has steadily increased with many Protestant and Orthodox Churches being joined, after the Second Vatican Council, by Roman Catholic theologians. The history of work on baptism, eucharist and ministry within the Faith and Order Commission of the World Council of Churches falls into two distinct periods: in the first the work was one of comparison between the views of the different Churches; this was followed in 1967 by the struggle to articulate a genuine doctrinal consensus between the Churches in the areas of Baptism, Eucharist and Ministry.

11. An important stage in the development of the text came in 1974 with the publication of the *Accra Text, One Baptism, One Eucharist and a Mutually Recognised Ministry*. The text demonstrated a growing convergence amongst the theologians of the Commission particularly in the areas of baptism and eucharist. It also witnessed to significant shifts in the understanding of the ordained ministry. More significant perhaps was the new process which encouraged the Churches to respond to the text and to receive its theological convergence. The Churches were invited to reflect on the work of their own theologians and to send back comments to Geneva, indicating how far the statements were consonant with their own beliefs. Careful analysis of the one hundred and forty or so replies highlighted areas calling for further work and a greater understanding between traditions. In particular the division between those who practise infant baptism and those who practise 'believers' baptism and the relation between *episkopé* and episcopacy became subjects for further work. The work between Accra

and Lima helped to move the statements from being statements of a small group of theologians to being statements of the Churches themselves.

12. The *Lima Text* is a completely revised text and differs significantly from the earlier *Accra Text*. It represents, as the Preface indicates, 'the significant theological convergence which the Faith and Order Commission has discerned and formulated'. The text is not a comprehensive formulation on the three matters covered. It deals mainly with particular points of misunderstanding and disagreements which have led to division. It does not represent full consensus.

Questions put to the Churches

13. The World Council of Churches has sent the *Lima Text* to all the Churches and invited them to answer four questions. The *first* is of particular importance and has complex and significant implications:

> the extent to which your Church can recognize in this text the faith of the Church through the ages.

The question does not ask whether we can recognize in the text the faith of Anglicanism. It would therefore not be appropriate simply to compare it with the historic formularies of the Church of England or any Provincial texts. The question involves the indentification and affirmation of the universal Christian tradition which has been mediated to us through the various traditions of all our Churches. Moreover, the World Council wishes to know the *extent* to which the Churches agree that the text expresses what each understands to be 'the faith of the Church through the ages'. This involves identifying where the *Lima Text* does not express the faith as it might, because it omits, over-emphasises, or otherwise needs to deal more adequately with particular issues. The *second* question concerns the implications of what the text says for relations with other Churches, in particular those who agree together that they can recognize it as an expression of what the Church understands to be 'the faith of the Church through the ages':

the consequences your Church can draw from this text for its relations and dialogues with other Churches, particularly with those Churches which also recognize the text as an expression of the apostolic faith.

The *third* question concerns other practical implications of what the text says for our own Church:

the guidance your Church can take from this text for its worship, educational, ethical and spiritual life and witness.

The *fourth* question concerns the ongoing agenda of the Faith and Order Commission itself:

the suggestions your Church can make for the ongoing work of Faith and Order as it relates the material of this text on Baptism, Eucharist and Ministry to its long range project *Towards the Common Expression of the Apostolic Faith Today*.

The Response of the Provinces of the Anglican Communion

THE RESPONSE PROCESS IN THE ANGLICAN COMMUNION

14. The *Lima Text* was referred by the World Council to its member Churches. Each Province of the Anglican Communion was asked to send its response direct to Geneva. This process has provided the Anglican Communion with an opportunity to bring together the Provincial responses and to consider how particular local circumstances affect Anglican answers to the question put to us by the World Council and also to see whether there is agreement in the Communion on this sacramental agenda.

15. The following analysis is based on responses from:
The Church of the Province of Southern Africa
The Holy Catholic Church in Japan (Nippon Sei Ko Kai)
The Church in Wales
The Scottish Episcopal Church
The Church of England
The Church of Ireland

The Anglican Church of Canada
The Episcopal Church of the USA
The Anglican Church of Australia
The Church of Melanesia
The Church of Province of New Zealand
The Province of the Southern Cone of America

These replies suggest, as in the case of those received in response to the *Final Report* of ARCIC that international ecumenical texts are more easily and swiftly handled in areas where translation of the text is not a problem and where resources for communication are more easily available. In order to reflect the mind of the world-wide Anglican Communion some thought needs to be given as how best to assist those Provinces that have particular difficulties in handling ecumenical texts. It needs to be noted that although official response from the Provinces was invited by the end of 1986 the process of reception is a much longer and widespread one.

16. No two Provinces have formulated their response in the same way. Geography, numerical size of a Province, as well as available theological and financial resources have determined what is possible in any one Province. Nevertheless, one striking feature in almost every Provincial process has been the degree of local parochial involvement in the study of the text. A number of Provinces mention also the involvement of theological colleges, the sharing in ecumenical study groups and the close linking of the *Lima Text* with the *Final Report* of ARCIC in the response process. In most Provinces a group of professional theologians has taken a major responsibility for preparing the final response. Provincial synods, diocesan and sometimes deanery synods have also been involved. Only one Province left the task entirely in the hands of a group of professional theologians. The Provincial accounts indicate that Anglicans are committed to involving clergy and laity in reflecting on doctrinal matters. Although bishops, as members of synods, have helped in forming the Provincial responses, few of the descriptions, apart from the one from the Church in

Wales, refer specifically to the oversight of the bishops in the process. The process of response has been an interesting one for Anglican self understanding. Although the World Council of Churches asked for an official response at 'the highest appropriate level of authority' the formulation of that response has been done on the basis of widespread study and consultation in most Provinces of the Communion.

The Overall Verdict

17. The general verdict emerging from the Provincial responses is that the *Lima Text* is balanced and comprehensive in the subjects it treats. All the responses express appreciation for the work of the Faith and Order Commission and acknowledge the achievement of the *Lima Text*. In the words of the response from the Church of Ireland: 'it is a positive document admirable in comprehensiveness, with an honesty of approach and economy of style'. The Episcopal Church of the USA says 'it is hard to exaggerate the importance of BEM'. The Church of England response applauds 'the remarkable theological convergence registered in all three texts and believes that it will be possible, following the direction of the text, to move further towards that consensus necessary to support the visible unity of the Church'.

18. Many of the Provincial responses agree that to an impressive degree 'the faith of the Church through the ages' can be recognised in the *Lima Text*. 'We recognize in this Text an appropriate expression of the Faith of the Church handed down through the ages from the Apostles' time' (the Church of Japan). The Episcopal Church of the USA, however, makes the point that the text is not an exhaustive treatment of the faith of the Church. There is, however, no agreement on which of the three texts is the most valuable. The Church of Melanesia finds only the baptism text satisfactory; the Episcopal Church of the USA also gives strongest approval to the baptism text; the Episcopal Church of Scotland finds the eucharist text most satisfactory while a number of Provinces agree that it is the minstry text that will need most work in the future.

19.   Many Provinces recognize the comprehensiveness of the text: the Episcopal Church of the USA refers to 'a wide and significant range of agreement . . . a range of theological opinion'; the Church of Australia, 'a pluralism which represents the pluralism of our own traditions'. So the *Lima Text* is taken to mirror the 'fair range of theological opinion within our own communion'. The Church of the Southern Cone of South America notes a danger in the text that each participant interprets the documents from his or her own perspective without there being a substantial agreement. In other words there is a possibility that every Church can read into it what it likes! However, the fact that in the response process so far different denominations have in fact produced opposing reactions to some elements in the text would suggest that such a view is hard to sustain.

20.   A number of Provinces set their comments on the subjects of baptism, eucharist and ministry within an acknowledgment of the type of text the *Lima Text* is, namely a convergence and not a consensus text. This means that more work needs to be done, particularly in the areas pointed to in the Commentaries of the *Lima Text*. Some Provinces also note and approve the method used by the Commission in forming the text, the attempt to go back behind the polarised divisions and to recapture together the Tradition of Scripture and the earliest years of the undivided Church and to express the Tradition together in the light of the traditions of all the Churches. The Church of England recognizes this method as characteristically Anglican and consonant with what is said in its own Declaration of Assent. The Declaration refers to the faith 'uniquely revealed in the Holy Scriptures and set forth in the historic formularies of the Church of England'. This faith has to be 'proclaimed afresh' in each generation. The Church of England response comments: 'it is, however, in dialogue with others, in the broader ecumenical community, that we come nearest to the perception of "the faith of the Church through the ages", as we learn to supplement each other's traditions'.

None of the Provincial responses set out simply to compare the *Lima Text* with Anglican formularies.

Preliminary Issues in Need of Articulation

21. The Provincial responses point to three underlying areas which need fuller treatment:

THE RELATION BETWEEN SCRIPTURE, TRADITION AND TRADITIONS

Comments suggest that the earlier work of the Faith and Order Commission on Scripture, Tradition and traditions which were set out in the *Montreal Report* of 1967 are not widely understood and have not generally been received. The results of the *Lima Text* could not have been reached without this earlier work on Scripture and Tradition.

THE NATURE OF SACRAMENTS

At least two Provinces miss a general statement by way of introduction on the nature of sacraments and their relation to the essential nature of the Church. 'The sacraments are described as "signs", but whether they are mere symbols or effective signs (instruments) does not explicitly emerge (cf Article XXV BCP)' (Church of Australia). While the Church of the Province of New Zealand also refers to the matter it goes on to point out that there is in fact sufficient instrumental language used of baptism, together with one very clear statement that baptism 'signifies and effects' participation in Christ's death and resurrection, for Anglicans to be content. Closely related to this is a question raised by the Episcopal Church of the USA. Are the non-sacramental bodies (e.g. the Friends, Salvation Army) excluded by this document from the ecclesial community?

AN ECCLESIOLOGICAL FRAMEWORK

A number of Provinces agree that the significant doctrinal convergences in the text would benefit from being set in an ecclesiological framework. However, a reading of the text does disclose the main lines of an ecumenical ecclesiology and in its response the Church of England tries to draw out the implicit ecclesiology lying behind each of the three parts of the text. We note that in response to a similar question from other denominations Max Thurian, responsible for collating the responses of the Churches to BEM, has written: 'The ecclesiology presupposed by the Lima document and thought of as that of the New Testament (which does not rule out institutional diversity), is definitely a 'sacramental' ecclesiology. The Church is the sign of God's presence and instrument of God's work in the world; it is the Body of Christ which unites believers by the word and sacraments; it is the temple of the Holy Spirit in which Christians are sanctified by faith and prayer'.

RESPONSE TO THE FIRST QUESTION: *the extent to which your Church can recognise in this text the faith of the Church through the ages.*

(A) The Baptism Text

GENERAL REFLECTIONS

22. There is a high degree of approval for what is claimed by the *Lima Text* for the meaning of baptism and for the fact that this is firmly anchored in the Bible. However, the Church of Ireland suggests that more emphasis might have been given to the traditional Anglican teaching on original sin (Articles IX, XXVIII), on baptism as 'grafting' us into the Body of Christ and the concept of 'adoption of sonship' by baptism. The Church of the Province of the Southern Cone, the Church in Wales and the Episcopal Church of Scotland agree that the theme of covenant needs to be developed in relation to the understanding of baptism. Further, the Church of the Province of Southern Cone suggests that too high claims are made in the text for what baptism is and what baptism does, which do not correspond to the reality of life. Certainly, if baptism is understood simply in terms of an external rite or ceremony it is easy to understand the reservations expressed by the Southern

Cone. This suggests that a greater clarity in the use of the term baptism in the *Lima Text* might have prevented any confusion.

GOD'S GIFT AND OUR RESPONSE

23. There is general approval of the delicate balance held between God's gracious gift to us and our response of faith. 'Baptism is both God's gift and our human response to that gift' (B8). The Episcopal Church in the USA suggests that, a better phrasing would be: 'baptism *involves* both God's gift and our human response to that gift'. There seems to be general agreement with the view expressed by the Church of Ireland that 'Lima deals with the relation of baptism and faith with a clarity that should be helpful to the confused'! All welcome the stress the *Lima Text* places on the proper context of baptism being within the believing community. The faith of the individual is not to be divorced from the faith of the Church. The Church of England expresses the view that Lima's balance between God's gift and our response of faith, together with the emphasis on the faith of the believing community, provides a basis for the reconciling of the two practices of infant baptism and 'believers' baptism within a unified Church.

THE BEGINNING OF A PROCESS

24. The Church of England's response welcomes the emphasis on baptism as a 'decisive beginning' in a process of life-long growth into Christ. This provides a basis for understanding the relationship between the different parts of the initiation process – baptism, confirmation/chrismation, first communion, Christian nurture. This is echoed in other responses which go on to draw out the practical implications of this for the Church's responsibility to nurture and develop baptismal faith both in the individual and in the life of the Church. The Church of the Province of New Zealand adds that some post-Reformation Anglican attempts to find a rationale for episcopal confirmation sit uneasily with BEM.

INFANT BAPTISM AND 'BELIEVERS' BAPTISM

25. A number of responses, like that of the Church of Australia question whether the contrast implied in the phrases,

'infant baptism' and 'believers baptism' is a correct one. 'Is not the proper alternative to the baptism of infants the baptism of those able to answer for themselves?' Both the Church of England and the Episcopal Church of Scotland make clear that although they have no wish to relinquish the practice of infant baptism themselves, nevertheless they understand believers' baptism to be the theological and liturgical model. This is closely tied to the question of so called 'indiscriminate' baptism. While many Provinces are aware of the problems and ambiguities, the Church of England's response seems to sum up for many Anglicans: 'it is a delicate matter to judge who should be baptised and who deferred, as no response is without ambiguity. On the one hand the text is right to warn of the offence which the indiscriminate practice of baptism can cause, where admission to baptism is granted to those who do not seem to have given evidence of wanting to be identified with Jesus Christ and his Church. On the other hand baptismal discipline may be so 'over discriminating' that those requesting baptism are required to provide unreasonable evidence of the authenticity of their faith'.

SPECIFIC QUESTIONS POSED TO ANGLICANS BY THE BAPTISMAL TEXT

26. The Provincial responses indicate that there are matters raised in the *Lima Text* which need particular consideration by Anglicans:

> the so called practice of indiscriminate 'infant baptism';
> the involvement of congregations in baptismal services;
> the eucharistic setting for baptism;
> Christian nurture of both the child and adult and the possibility of exploring the ancient order of the catechumenate;
> the challenge to the Anglican pattern of interposing a separate rite of confirmation between baptism and participation in the eucharist.

The *Lima Text* also raises new issues relating to baptismal practice which need further study:

> the Episcopal Church of the USA and the Church in

Canada both draw attention to the fact that some Churches, or individuals within Churches, baptise in a different formula from the classical one, but still understand them as administering Christian Baptism. The Church of Canada mentions specifically the request of some for a gender-free formula, 'Creator, Redeemer and Sanctifier'.

the relation of baptism in water and baptism in the Holy Spirit. The Church of the Province of New Zealand says 'there is no attempt to relate baptism in water to what is known in pentecostal and some charismatic circles as "baptism in the Holy Spirit" and in an ecumenical document this is a serious defect'.

(B) The Eucharist Text

GENERAL REFLECTIONS

27. Most of the Provincial responses find the *Lima Text* on the eucharist biblically based, grounded in recent biblical scholarship and representing 'the faith of the Church through the ages'. The Church of England adds to this a particular welcome for the Trinitarian basis of the text. Hesitations and qualifications are offered within this overall affirmation of the text. The Church of the Province of Melanesia, however, writes that 'we appreciate the balance of the treatment of the different aspects of the eucharist text, but cannot recognize in it the faith of the Church through the ages, as the eucharist has been the centre of bitter controversy.' This is not expounded in their response.

THE CENTRAL ACT OF WORSHIP

28. There is wholehearted approval for the insistence of the *Lima Text* that the eucharist is the central act of the Church's worship and that it should be celebrated at least once a week. Some Provinces note that this insistence ought to be discussed openly by Anglicans as they prepare to move into relationships of closer fellowship with other Christians. The text asserts that the eucharist as a central act of the Church's worship 'always includes both word and sacrament'. While the reading of the

Scriptures and the preaching of the Word are a part of the proclamation, the entire eucharistic action is also to be understood as a proclamation of the Word. The Episcopal Church of the USA would like to have seen a further development of this, particularly of how the Word is integral to the sacrament.

THE EPICLESIS

29. While some Provinces welcome the emphasis the *Lima Text* places upon the role of the Holy Spirit and the *epiclesis* in the eucharist, the Church of Ireland is not alone in suggesting that the appeal for the restoration in the liturgy of the invocation of the Spirit on both the community and upon the elements goes beyond Anglican tradition as that tradition has been expressed in their own formularies. 'The suggestion that the whole action of the eucharist has an "*epikletic*" character would seem to be more in line with the emphasis in our own formularies on the spiritual character of the service as a whole. (We note, however, that the double *epiclesis* was to be found in the text of 1549!)'

EUCHARIST AND SACRIFICE

30. Most Provinces welcome the attempt of the *Lima Text* to avoid the old controversies that centred around both sacrifice and presence. The Episcopal Church of the USA believes that the text does not gloss over the issues but transcends the usual terms of controversies. There is a range of opinion about whether the biblical concept of *anamnesis* is made to bear more weight than it is able to carry. Both the Church of England and the Church of Canada, for example, appear satisfied on the point while the Church of Australia suggests the concept needs examination. The response from the Church of the Province of the Southern Cone suggests that 'memorial' is an inadequate translation of *anamnesis*, 'commemoration' should have been used.

THE PRESENCE OF CHRIST IN THE EUCHARIST

31. A number of responses support the text in relating the presence of Christ to the whole eucharistic celebration and not

only to the eucharistic elements. Again there is a difference of opinion over how satisfactory the text is on the subject of the presence and the elements. The Church of England is not alone in believing that the text has maintained the right balance when it says 'while Christ's real presence in the eucharist does not depend on the faith of the individual, all agree that to discern the body and blood of Christ, faith is required'. Further, 'the text is faithful to the Church through the ages when it upholds the real presence of Christ in the eucharist and his body and blood truly received in the bread and wine, without demanding further agreement on the mode of that presence in the elements.' The report from the Episcopal Church of Scotland points to the compatibility of the Lima statement on the presence with what is said in ARCIC. ARCIC contains a double emphasis on the presence of Christ in the elements and the living encounter with Christ in the believer. However, the Church of Australia is concerned that the text does not allow room for those in the Anglican tradition who see Christ's presence as being found in the faithful reception of the elements. 'As touching the presence of Christ in the Eucharist, the Anglican tradition has encompassed the views of those who see Christ's presence as being specifically linked with the elements and those who see Christ's presence as being found in the faithful reception of those elements. This later viewpoint does not appear to find expression in the E section of BEM, save, possibly, in E15 and Commentary.'

RESERVATION

32. What is believed about the presence of Christ in the eucharist is closely related to the practice of reservation and the disposal of the elements. A number of replies show that the Anglican practice of reservation is for the communion of the sick and those not present at the celebration of the community. All that is not so required ought to be consumed. However, the Church of Province of the Southern Cone suggests that 'reservation is a mistaken practice'. The practice of both consumption of the consecrated elements and reservation are particularly relevant issues in our relations with other

Churches. The Church in Wales sums it up when it suggests that 'it would do much to allay unnecessary suspicions if Churches engaged in the quest for unity had a more or less uniform practice with regard to the consecrated elements remaining over'.

THE ELEMENTS OF BREAD AND WINE

33. On the question of the use of elements other than bread and wine in the eucharist raised in a commentary on the *Lima Text* the Church of the Province of New Zealand recognizes the need for further study. 'This may well be raised within our own Province which includes the diocese of Polynesia.'

THE CELEBRANT

34. There is agreement amongst the Provinces that they would wish to see the text make clear that while at every eucharist the true president is indeed Christ, an ordained priest ought to preside.

THE ETHICAL IMPLICATIONS

35. Many of the Provinces approve the way the *Lima Text* links the celebration of the eucharist to the need for the renewal of human community both within the Church and the world. 'We find much to approve in the way that Lima keeps the eucharist firmly anchored in the reality of the Church's life in the world. The community reconciled in the eucharist becomes in turn the instrument of reconciliation. The sharing of the eucharist challenges us to fight against injustice or oppression. The love of Christ which we experience sends us out in the service of human need'. (The Church of Ireland).

(C) The Ministry Text

GENERAL REFLECTIONS

36. The Provincial responses all recognize that the ministry text is the furthest from consensus of the three texts. Nevertheless, they acknowledge the significant advances in the understanding of the ordained ministry which have been made in the broad ecumenical forum of the World Council. The

Episcopal Church of the USA sums it up in this way: 'On the whole we found this a helpful and thoughtful section, although it also presents many unresolved difficulties'. Both the theology of the ministry and the practice of ordained ministry set out in the *Lima Text* are recognized to contain challenges for Anglicans. This is particularly so in relation to our diaconal and episcopal expressions of ministry.

THE MINISTRY OF THE WHOLE PEOPLE OF GOD

37.   The text is thought rightly to set what it has to say about ordained ministry within the context of the ministry of the whole people of God and to see the Church's ministry as deriving from and dependent on Christ. Some Provinces wish for a fuller treatment of the ministry of all the baptised and the diversity of ministries as a proper balance to what is said about ordained ministry.

THE THREEFOLD PATTERN

38.   There is general welcome for the handling of the threefold ministry. While the *Lima Text* makes clear that no single pattern can be found in the New Testament, it nevertheless regards the threefold pattern as the one which may serve today as an expression of the unity we seek and also as a means of achieving it. At the same time the Church of Canada points out the importance in Lima of the recognition that episcopal, presbyteral and diaconal functions are exercised by those Churches that do not have a threefold order. This is the thought developed in the Anglican–Reformed dialogue and is important for unity negotiations. What is said about the functions and manner of exercise of the three forms of ministry is seen to challenge Anglican practice radically. The response from the Episcopal Church of the USA looks for more on the interrelation of the three orders of ministry as they function together on behalf of the Church. There is no clarity in describing the ecclesial structures in which they function. 'Is the basic structure of the Church a diocese or a local congregation?' and 'how do presbyters share in the councils of the Church?'

APOSTOLICITY AND APOSTOLIC SUCCESSION

39. The Church of England's response recognizes that what is said in the *Lima Text* about apostolicity and apostolic succession breaks new ground and is important for bringing together episcopal and non-episcopal Churches. Apostolicity and apostolic succession are understood in relation to faithfulness to the teaching and mission of the Apostles. 'Bishops become one of the ways, together with the transmission of the Gospel and the life of the community, in which the apostolic tradition of the Church was expressed'. This succession was seen as serving, symbolising and guarding the continuity of apostolic faith, mission and the communion of the Church. On the basis of such an understanding many of the Provinces acknowledge the challenge to non-episcopal Churches to consider taking episcopacy into their systems and equally the challenge to episcopal Churches to reform the expression of episcopal ministry.

THE PRIESTHOOD OF THE MINISTRY

40. The response from both England and Scotland welcomes Lima's expression of the priesthood of the ordained ministry which is not, they both suggest, inconsistent with what the ARCIC statement asserts about the priesthood of the ordained ministry.

PERSONAL, COLLEGIAL AND COMMUNAL FORMS OF MINISTRY

41. Several of the Provinces recognize the importance of what is said in the *Lima Text* about personal, collegial and communal forms of ministry that need to be expressed at every level of the Church's life. This is a significant contribution to the study of structures of decision making and teaching authoritatively. It has relevance for the emerging structures of authority in the Anglican Communion, particularly at the universal level. The Church of the Province of New Zealand suggests that the *Lima Text* does not spell out sufficiently the interrelatedness of the ordained ministry and the laity. They point out that this is

worked out in their own structures in synodical government at diocesan and Provincial level.

THE ORDINATION OF WOMEN

43. Almost all the Provinces comment on the lack of space devoted to the subject of the ordination of women. Anglicans would wish for much more guidance. The Church of Australia, for example, comments that 'it would be helpful if biblical and theological reasons endorsing the ordination of women could be set out explicitly with special concern both for the inner unity of those Churches which are considering the ordination of women as well as the implications for the wider unity of the Christian community as a whole.' Both the Church of Canada and the Episcopal Church of the USA make the point that more needs to be said about the ordination of women, 'not only as a problem to be discussed as a possible obstacle to union, but as a positive good and appropriate to the human expression of the fullness of Christ's priesthood in the Church'.

THE OFFICE OF A UNIVERSAL PRIMATE

44. At least three Provinces point to the lack of reference to a universal primate as a service for unity in a united Church. They suggest that work on this issue in the multilateral context provided by Faith and Order would provide an important term of reference for bilateral dialogues.

45. The overall verdict of the Provinces on the first question put to the Churches is that the *Lima Text* does to a very great extent witness to the faith of the Church through the ages. At the same time there is recognition that the *Lima Text* is not an exhaustive treatment of that faith, and that there are matters upon which consensus has not yet been reached. There is encouragement for the Faith and Order Commission in dialogue with the Churches to continue the convergence process.

RESPONSE TO THE SECOND QUESTION: *the consequences your Church can draw from this text for its relations and* *dialogues with other Churches, particularly with those Churches which also recognise the text as an expression of the apostolic faith.*

46. Almost all the Provinces recognise that if Anglicans and those of other Churches can recognise in the *Lima Text* 'the faith of the Church through the ages' this must have some implications for the relationships between the Churches. It makes no sense to give a positive answer to question 1 and to continue to live in separation. This is particularly seen to be the implication of the baptism text. The Episcopal Church of Scotland says 'we welcome warmly section 6 on Baptism as incorporation into the Body of Christ, which though axiomatic for many has implications for ecumenism which have not been grasped by the vast majority of Christians. We wish to develop the idea that our common baptism is a "basic bond of unity", in the light of the High Priestly prayer of Jesus (John 17) that Christians be actually united within the Godhead, i.e. that Church unity is first and foremost a relationship between one Christian and another'. The Church of the Province of Southern Africa commenting on the *Lima Text*'s insistence that baptism is the 'basic bond of unity' says: 'this means that our unity in Christ is itself a gift of God, so that baptism indeed is a "call to the Churches to overcome their divisions and visibly manifest their fellowship".' The Church of England indicates that each part of the *Lima Text* raises an agenda to be taken up with Churches in England: the baptism text provides a basis for resuming conversations with the Baptist Union, and raises questions about the practice of joint confirmations in Local Ecumenical Projects; the eucharist text leads to questions about eucharistic hospitality and common joint celebrations of the eucharist; the ministry text suggests a renewed discussion amongst English Churches on the subject of the reconciliation of ministries and reflection upon the more recent development of parallel ordinations. Above all the *Lima Text* is recognised as providing the Churches with an unprecedented opportunity to re-commit themselves to the goal of visible unity. And the Church of England suggests that together the Churches might find a way of celebrating the convergence of

the *Lima Text* at a local, regional and international level. 'Symbolic acts can have a lasting significance in relationships between hitherto divided communions . . . all too often we are left recounting the failures rather than celebrating the signs of hope which are already here'.

RESPONSE TO THE THIRD QUESTION: *the guidance your Church can take from this text for its ethical, educational, ethical and spiritual life and witness*

47. Perhaps the most striking thing about the Provincial responses is the emphasis they lay on the challenge of the *Lima Text* to Anglicans to reform their own lives. The *Lima Text* is seen as challenging Anglicans to put their own house in order. Again and again the responses point out the inconsistencies between what Anglicans say they believe and how they live out their belief in life. This is seen to be true in the practice of baptism, eucharist and ministry. As we have already noted the baptism text raises questions about so called 'indiscriminate baptism', responsibility for Christian nurture and the relation of baptism, confirmation, first communion: the eucharist text raises questions about eucharistic hospitality and eucharistic sharing, the need to live out more faithfully the belief that the eucharist is the feast where the Church recognises the signs of renewal already at work in the world, where, united with Christ in a special way it prays for the world, and is the centre from which Christians go out renewed by the power of the Spirit to work as reconcilers in a broken world: the ministry text raises questions about the theology and practice of episcopacy in the Anglican Communion, the use of the diaconate, the complementarity of women and men in ministry and the relation of personal, collegial and communal forms of ministry.

48. Several of the Provincial responses take up the implications of what is said in the introduction to the *Lima Text* about the distinction between official response and reception. The request to give official response to the *Lima Text* from 'the highest appropriate level of authority' raises a question for

Anglicans. The Church of England refers to the matter in this way: 'For Anglicans the way of dialogue through the Communion is important in forming the mind of the Church. However, it is precisely this strength of Anglicanism that is also a weakness, for how do we know when the Anglican Communion has formed its mind and what organ or what person(s) is to announce that common mind to our partners in dialogue? . . . the Anglican Communion is striving to understand the relationships of Provinces to one another and the process by which common decisions, which are binding on all, are to be made'. The process of responding officially to both multilateral and bilateral texts is forcing the Anglican Communion to consider its own identity and to change and be changed in the process. A number of Provinces go on to underline the importance of an ongoing process of reception of the theological convergences of the text, acknowledging what this means in terms of an investment of time and energy in getting the text studied as widely as possible.

RESPONSE TO THE FOURTH QUESTION: *the suggestions your Church can make for the ongoing work of Faith and Order as it relates the material of this text on Baptism, Eucharist and Ministry to its long range research project Towards the Common Expression of the Apostolic Faith Today.*

49. Among the suggestions offered by the Provinces for the future work of the Faith and Order Commission are the following:

the developing of those matters on which consensus has not yet been reached and which are referred to in the commentaries of the *Lima Text* e.g., the relation of the parts of the initiation process; the status of the celebrant of the Eucharist; the priesthood of the ordained ministry; the ordination of women to the priesthood; universal primacy;

work on those underlying matters mentioned in paragraph 21 of this chapter: the relation of Scripture, Tradition and traditions; the nature of sacraments and, in particular, the ecclesiology that lies behind the *Lima Text*;

the deepening work on the study *Towards the Common Confession of the Apostolic Faith Today*. The Church of the Province of New Zealand adds 'we would prefer the title "A Common Contemporary Expression of Apostolic Faith" because we want to recognize the pluralism which occurs in the New Testament, affirm the need for continuing with apostolic faith, yet seek also to find a contemporary expression of that faith';

a resuming of the earlier study *How Does the Church Teach Authoritatively Today?* in the light of what the Ministry text says about personal, collegial and communal ministry;

the study on *the Unity of the Church and the Renewal of Human Community* is seen as providing an essential context for the search for the visible unity of the Church. The study points to the relationship between Church, world, Kingdom and holds together the unity and mission of the Church. The unity of the Church is not an end in itself but in a broken and divided world is called to be 'prophetic sign', 'instrument', and 'first fruits' of the eschatological Kingdom. This study needs to inform all the other work of the Faith and Order Commission.

Conclusion

50. The collation of the Provincial responses to *Baptism, Eucharist and Ministry* was not asked for by the World Council of Churches. The individual Provinces were invited to send their replies direct to Geneva. Nevertheless, it is clearly of value and importance that the Anglican Communion should bring together the Provincial replies and consider what implications these responses have both for the life of the Communion itself and also for our relations with other Churches. Further, the simultaneous drawing together of these responses and those to the *Final Report* of ARCIC helps to set the consensus and convergence of that bilateral dialogue within the convergence of the wider ecumenical movement.

51. On the basis of this collation of responses from 12 Provinces the ACC may wish to consider:

ways of eliciting responses from those Provinces which have not yet replied to the request of the World Council of Churches in order to form a more comprehensive view of the Anglican Communion on the matter;

ways of assisting Provinces which have particular difficulties in translating, interpreting and disseminating the results of the texts in their area;

how to encourage an ongoing process of credible reception of the convergences in the *Lima Text* in the life of the Communion;

what the process of response and reception described in the Provincial replies have to tell Anglicans about structures of authority and decision making in the Anglican Communion;

the particular issues raised by the Provincial responses which merit internal Anglican reflection. The meeting of ecumenical officers and bishops highlighted a number of such issues. A study of Anglican statements on sources and structures of authority might usefully be made and considered in relation to the Montreal Statement on *Scripture, Tradition and traditions* as well as what is being said in the area in other bilateral dialogues. The stress in the *Lima Text* on baptism into the body of Christ, the community of the Church, raises the question of the implications this has for Church membership as it is expressed in particular denominations and how is the anomaly of one baptism and different denominations to be overcome. The very considerable convergence in the understanding of the eucharist text raises questions for Anglicans about eucharistic hospitality and eucharistic sharing. What is said in the ministry text about both diaconal and episcopal forms of ministry raise questions for the Anglican expression of these forms of ministry. Similarly, the convergences of the text on ministry have implications for the mutual recognition of ministries on the way to the reconciliation of ministries. And the reflections of the *Lima Text* as an expression of personal, collegial and communal forms of ministry at all levels of the Church's life raises questions for the developing structures within the Anglican Communion;

the implications for the life and witness of the Anglican Communion in the way in which the *Lima Text* relates the celebration of the sacraments to the breaking down of the divisions of the human community both within the Church and in the world;

those areas of study which the Faith and Order Commission of the WCC should be encouraged to pursue. The meeting of ecumenical officers and bishops noted that the Provincial responses supported the development of work on the programme *Towards the Common Expression of the Apostolic Faith Today* and *The Unity of the Church and the Renewal of Human Community* but saw as particularly pressing the need for the Faith and Order Commission to resume work on structures of decision making and teaching authoritatively;

what special opportunities for dialogue between Anglicans and other Churches have been opened up within the worldwide ecumenical response process. The meeting of ecumenical officers and bishops was aware that the Anglican Communion is engaged at the present time in a number of international bilateral dialogues. There are, however, many other Churches with whom dialogues would be creative. It may be that bilateral meetings at national, regional or international levels should be encouraged to compare denominational responses to the *Lima Text*. In particular, Anglicans have no international bilateral dialogue with either Methodists or Baptists although in many areas they work closely together in Co-operating Parishes and Local Ecumenical Projects.

9
The Growth of New Churches

It is sometimes suggested that enthusiasm for ecumenical dialogue is a sign of the decay of a Church and that joining two small dead Churches produces one large dead Church. Without assenting to such criticism we need to beware lest when the mainline Churches have achieved visible unity, we suddenly discover that the majority of vital Christians and Churches are outside it! For this reason, in our survey of the ecumenical scene we need to take cognisance of the existence and growth of thousands of independent Churches and groups with whom Anglicans are often not in dialogue, yet which have already become in many cases mainstream established Churches with strong, young leadership and growth. The following observations are based on two out of many types of such Churches, namely, the Pentecostal Churches and the Independent Churches of Africa. Some obviously are newer than others.

At their best the Pentecostal-type new Churches (to take this group first) have come into existence and grown phenomenally because of perceived failings in mainline Churches, e.g. coldness in worship, failure to take the gospel challenges seriously, failure to live by the power of the Holy Spirit, to manifest his fruit and utilise his gifts, obsession with lifeless tradition, etc. A further motivation for the formation of such denominations and groups has been a particular interpretation of certain Scriptural passages concerning baptism, the Holy Spirit, ministry and so forth.

Christians of other branches of the Church can thank God for the impact made by the neo-Pentecostal renewal movement upon the whole Church, as evidenced by greater freedom and joy in praise and worship, more frequent conversions of Church members, increased lay leadership and mutual caring, a taking seriously of the ministry of healing and of the gifts of the Spirit, sacrificial giving including tithing, the growth of Bible study and prayer house groups, concern about evangelism, etc.

As the Lambeth Conference declared in 1978:

> The Holy Spirit has been manifesting his presence and power anew in the Church today. In various parts of the world, and not least where there has been severe pressure or threat of trouble, we have seen a kindling of true discipleship, evangelical zeal, and a growth both of numbers and spiritual power. Thus the 'renewal movements', including the charismatic movement, have become a feature of the life of many different Communions, our own included, and for this we thank God (p. 111).

The movement has often been followed by division in the household of God, the blame for which can doubtless be shared in various proportions between adherents and opponents, although the rigidity and apparent judgmentalism of some 'new converts' has made relationships difficult.

Although we can welcome the participation of many ministers of 'charismatic' Churches in ecumenism and although there is sometimes much greater doctrinal common ground than was expected, further study together concerning 're-baptism', the nature of the Church, the socio-political involvement of Christians and indeed a whole range of theological and pastoral matters is urgently needed.

Dialogue is to be encouraged, though it is not as easy to pursue with house-group Churches as with established neo-Pentecostal denominations. In most cases the need for a comprehensive Church and structural visible unity is not perceived, though the experience of the given unity in the Spirit at common gatherings is deeply felt.

The second group of 'new' Churches may be called the Independent Churches (e.g. of Africa and South America). Some of these may have come into being through personal jealousies and leadership rivalries (see 1 Corinthians 3). Many however (e.g. in Southern Africa and Kenya) are expressions of a desire to introduce cultural ethos, racial and nationalist feelings, political aspirations, and/or ancestral beliefs into the life and worship of the Church. The wish for freedom from existing authority can be another factor, together with the need for greater freedom of expression in worship.

Anglicans need to examine what defects in their own life and practice and those of other historic Churches have enabled the independent sects to acquire the following that they have. In its self-examination Anglicans would do well to consider whether all the independent Churches do not challenge us:

(a) to affirm the Biblical basis of the ecumenical movement and its aims more strongly;

(b) to lay more emphasis in the Anglican Communion on inculturation;

(c) to express a greater confidence in the gospel and in evangelism;

(d) to recognise the importance of Christians meeting in small groups;

(e) to lay greater emphasis on the ministry to which every Church member is called through baptism.

(f) to recognise the need of individuals for pastoral love and for community – not always obtainable in our existing parochial structures.

Dialogue with a view to joint mission and action in local situations is taking place in some areas and is clearly to be encouraged.

A good deal of research, analysis and sociological study has doubtless been done by the WCC, universities and other bodies. The ACC is requested to assist Provinces to discover such study material. Bishops are respectfully asked to commend such material for study with a view to deepening relations with the main groups of Pentecostal and Independent Churches.

10

Visit to the Ecumenical Centre, Geneva, by some Participants in the Anglican Ecumenical Consultation, 2 – 5 February 1987

A party consisting of 12 participants in the Ecumenical Consultation at West Wickham subsequently travelled to Geneva to visit the Ecumenical Centre, which houses the staffs of the World Council of Churches, the Lutheran World Federation, the World Alliance of Reformed Churches, the Conference of European Churches, together with representatives of the Ecumenical Patriarchate, the Moscow Patriarchate, Presbyterian Church USA, and the World Methodist Council. During the visit the party was welcomed by the Old Catholic parish of St Germain in the city, and also by Emmanuel Episcopal Church and Holy Trinity Church.

In an intense two-day programme, we were able to meet most of the organisations within the Centre, while concentrating mainly on the World Council itself. The WCC operates in three Units, roughly corresponding to the three movements which have coalesced into the Council, Faith and Order, the International Missionary Council – now Commission on World Mission and Evangelism (CWME) – and the organisation originally formed for the rehabilitation of European Churches after the Second World War, which has now grown into the Commission on Inter-Church Aid, Refugee and World Service (CICARWS). The funding of these agencies is various – a portion coming from central Church funds, some from Mission Boards and Agencies, while some member Churches of WCC look to CICARWS to administer and operate their development and relief funding, a truly complex operation representing a variety of interests and funding sources. The General Secretariat has the task of co-ordinating the multiform activities of the Council. The Council has some 350 member Churches, which in itself leads to a complex operation to achieve adequate and fair representation at Assemblies.

The World Council is an instrument of the Churches to bring them into closer relation with each other in a movement whose aim is to bring local Churches, themselves truly united, into conciliar relation. Membership implies commitment to this goal, and the mutual commitment of Churches to each other. Member Churches have developed in many different contexts and cultures, speaking many languages, and the World Council is an essential organ to enable Churches to speak to each other and develop mutual understanding, moving from the paroikia into the oikumene.

There are eight Anglican members of staff in various programme units, together with others in support roles. We were immensely indebted to the Anglican staff in setting up the programme and helping to interpret it to us. Dr John Pobee, working with the Programme for Theological Education, opened with an orientation session, in which he suggested that we should have three questions uppermost during our visit. What contribution have Anglicans made to the Ecumenical Movement? Our continuing contribution depended on Anglican insights, which raised the question 'what is our identity?' Finally we should ask 'what have we to contribute?'.

The World Council has four overarching concerns – Gospel and Culture, Justice Peace and the Integrity of Creation, Spirituality, and a Vital and Coherent Theology. These were intended to give some shape to the Council's work. He then asked, what do Anglicans do about spirituality? If we are the Church of the Via Media, what has this to say to the Ecumenical Movement? At the practical level, are we offering and supporting staff in the WCC? Finally, are we using the resources of the WCC?

After two days, during which staff presented their concerns, hopes and expectations, we met with the General Secretariat to discuss impressions. One of our party remarked that he was reminded of a Stephen Leacock character who got on his horse and galloped off in all directions. What was the overall aim and purpose of all this activity? We were reminded of the overarching concerns, but no clear picture emerged.

Perhaps we had been standing too close. We need to think of the ways in which the WCC has influenced the climate in which all of us live and move and have our being. The Faith and Order Commission has produced *Baptism, Eucharist and Ministry*, a remarkable instance of theological convergence. Its future programme plots a steady course to the conciliarity which we seek. The missionary movement has so developed that the voice of Churches in six continents is now clearly heard through the work of the World Council. Tambaram, Lund, New Delhi, Uppsala, Nairobi, Bangkok, Melbourne and Vancouver mark the gatherings which have entered deeply into the consciousness of the Churches. The Programme to Combat Racism, the Church of the Poor, Conscientization, the cry for Justice and Peace have outraged and challenged the Churches of the affluent world, but the World Council has enabled that challenge to be heard. In many ways a Babel of voices which has led us all to reflect more deeply about the Good News and the Kingdom. There are those who complain of theology by slogans, jargon, shallow thinking, but the waters have been stirred.

It remains to say something of the kaleidoscope of impressions received.

Father Kenith David from South Africa spoke of Urban Rural Mission. Through his network they were in touch with 5,500 basic groups employing the action-reflection method. However poor and underprivileged the group, certain facts emerged.

1. There was an expressed need for community, the alternative to which was destruction.
2. God was a common factor – sometimes blamed as the cause of their plight, sometimes praised for the strength and hope He gave.
3. Pain was the common experience, sometimes hunger,

sometimes lack of peace, sometimes physical and violent. Whatever the cause, pain was prevalent.
4. In all of this there was longing and hope for justice.

In all of this, they know that politics features. URM saw its task as helping people recognize their pain, helping them analyse why they are in pain, and to move from individual to collective action. Knowledge of others in the same situation is essential and through such conscientization it becomes possible to build solidarity and the capacity to solve problems. URM had moved far from the early days of industrial mission, but felt that it had failed to challenge the traditional missionary structures which still seemed to suffer from a separation of Word and action in mission.

The 1989 Conference on World Mission and Evangelism

This was expected to take place in San Antonio, Texas. Already CWME was beginning to plan from the bottom up. Through member Churches, National and Regional Councils they are seeking to involve the grass roots. Participation begins now, to be brought together in 1989, hopefully enabling the Church to move in new directions. The enthusiasm and energy of WCC staff cannot be questioned. The response of the local Church is our concern, to do all we can to ensure maximum participation. Through staff visits to all parts of the world, they have to encourage group discussion. There will be a series of consultations on the meaning of evangelism and they expect that preparation involving all sections of society to be in full swing by March 1988.

One project is a poster competition for children between the ages of 8 – 12 on Justice, Peace and the Integrity of Creation. One of our group wondered what these words meant to this age group and it was explained that parents and teachers were expected to discuss with children the meaning of these words.

The main themes of the Conference: 1. One living faith, one living God – Unity in Mission. 2. Participating in Struggle and Suffering. 3. The earth is the Lord's – with special emphasis on land. 4. Mission and community. 5. Worship.

The Ecumenical Decade of the Church in Solidarity with Women

Anna Karin Hammar, the Swedish Director of Women in Church and Society, said that the Central Committee had approved this programme. The UNESCO decade for women had not really reached down to the general situation of women, and the Church with a predominance of women could use their resources in Church reorganisation with a more positive result.

She pointed out that even within the Church pattern of life, the nearer an organisation is to the home, the greater the participation of women in programme and decision making. Although in most societies women had been subordinate in the past, theoretically this was no longer the case in the North and was being challenged in the South, yet little had changed when it came to power sharing because of the prevailing structures in society.

Education and Renewal of Church Life

Acting on the conviction that 'all ministry is Christ's Ministry and all are called to ministry' we were shown Programme for Theological Education's concern for aspects of Ministerial Formation.

Young people had to be freed from paternal/maternal dominance in the life of Church and society. What was the theological agenda by which they could be empowered for participation in Christ's ministry? In the educational task of the Church, the emphasis was on the ecumenical nature of education, and the aim was to enable people to 'Act and think locally with global vision.'

Theological Education was increasingly aware of one world, different cultures, and the search for authentic contextualisation of the Gospel must go on. In all this the question was how the Unit can co-operate with Churches in bringing the enormous resources of knowledge gained in the WCC through years of international, inter-Church, inter-cultural experience to enable local Churches to reach forward in the mission to which God calls them in their different localities.

The Unit spoke of its financial limitations, wryly commenting that the unit was 'The one department Churches do not put money into'.

Faith and Order

This sub-unit has a very full programme collating and surveying the responses of Churches to BEM. No other World Council document has attracted such fully responsible consideration. All the responses will be published during the coming two years. The Commission will have to devote further time to consideration of some of the issues raised by Churches. At present it is also working on 'The Common Expression of the Apostolic Faith Today' and has been asked to play a major role in the 'Justice, Peace and Integrity of Creation' programme. As a result, its third thrust, Structures of Common Decision Making is not receiving the attention it deserves.

CICARWS

This unit expressed its concern that governments were using spectacular fund raising efforts such as Band Aid as an excuse for withdrawing from development aid projects. They also noted that traditional agencies were experiencing a drop in income, and that development projects starved of funds were turning to them for resources which they no longer had to offer. Although there was no time to discuss the mounting world debt crisis which is preventing capital formation in developing countries, it is clear that all Churches have to consider how they can appeal to conscience to resist the robbing of the poor nations by the rich.

Staffing

Vacancies on WCC Staff are circulated to member Churches. Do Anglican Provinces seriously consider what resources of personnel they have to offer, and possibly more important, how they can reintegrate ex-staff members into their structures? We are losing out on people who have an unprecedented experience to offer, even though it may be somewhat disturbing.

Parallel Thrusts

The Communion is developing various networks – Refugees, Peace, Youth, etc. Are we satisfied that we are making use of the immense resources on offer by the WCC, and equally important, are we contributing to those resources?

Spirituality

This has been identified, after the experience of the last Assembly in Vancouver, as a major area of World Council work. Anglicans contribute to the worship life of the Centre. Bishop John Taylor gave a series of Lenten addresses last year, but the nature of the community in the Centre rules out a regular sacramental life, nor would this be desirable until there is much greater clarity on the issue. It was good that members of our party were invited to celebrate the Eucharist during our visit, and that we could extend hospitality to members of other Churches present.

Anglicans on the World Council staff share in the life of the two Anglican Churches – Holy Trinity and Emmanuel Episcopal Church – as well as the Old Catholic Church of St Germain. There is a growing sense of common purpose between these Churches and a realisation of the role they can play with regard to the Centre. In a city where the greater part of the population are strangers, Anglicans can do much to incarnate their diversity in their eucharistic communities.

Christian World Communions

We met with the representatives of the Ecumenical Patriarchate and the Moscow Patriarchate, the Lutheran World
Federation and the World Alliance of Reformed Churches.
This opened up another world which we did not have time to
investigate fully.

Finally, we would wish to thank all those who gave
generously of their time and concern to welcome twelve
Anglican pilgrims and to share their enthusiasm, dedication
and something of their frustrations in the service of
ecumenism.

Participants in the Anglican Ecumenical Consultation

The Right Reverend Edward Buckle★
Vice-Chairman, Ecumenical Section,
Lambeth Conference 1988

The Most Reverend Donald Caird★
Archbishop of Dublin

The Most Reverend Peter Carnley
Archbishop of Perth

The Right Reverend Joseph Dadson★
Bishop of Tamale and Sunyani

The Reverend Canon Christopher Hill
Co-Secretary, Anglican-Roman Catholic
International Commission

The Right Reverend Edward Jones
Bishop of Indianapolis

The Right Reverend Misaeri Kauma★
Bishop of Namirembe

The Right Reverend Michael Nazir-Ali
Co-ordinator of Studies for the Lambeth Conference

The Reverend Dr William Norgren
Ecumenical Officer, Episcopal Church of the USA

The Right Reverend Kenneth Oram★
Bishop of Grahamstown

The Most Reverend Michael Peers★
Primate of Canada, Chairman, Ecumenical Section,
Lambeth Conference 1988

The Reverend Brian Prideaux★
Ecumenical Officer, Anglican Church of Canada

The Reverend Canon Martin Reardon (Convenor)
Secretary, Board for Mission and Unity, Church of England

Mrs Mary Tanner★
Theological Secretary, Board for Mission and Unity,
Church of England

The Very Reverend Hugh Wybrew★
Co-Secretary, Anglican–Orthodox Joint
Doctrinal Discussions

The Reverend William Taylor, Archbishop of Canterbury's
Adviser on Orthodox Affairs,
visited the meeting for two days.

Anglican Consultative Council

The Reverend George Braund, Ecumenical Secretary★

Ms Vanessa Wilde, Secretary★

★Participants in the visit to the Ecumenical Centre, Geneva

List of Abbreviations Used in This Report

ACC	Anglican Consultative Council
AOJDD	Anglican–Orthodox Joint Doctrinal Discussions
ARCIC I	Anglican–Roman Catholic International Commission
ARCIC II	Anglican–Roman Catholic International Commission II (1982-)
BEM	*Baptism, Eucharist and Ministry*, published by the World Council of Churches
CICARWS	Commission on Inter-Church Aid, Refugee and World Service
CHP	Church House Publishing
CWME	Commission on World Mission and Evangelism
LWF	Lutheran World Federation
PTE	Programme for Theological Education
SPCK	Society for Promoting Christian Knowledge
URM	Urban Rural Mission
WARC	World Alliance of Reformed Churches
WCC	World Council of Churches